VALUE CREATION THINKING

9/12/2016

BARTLEY J. MADDEN

Mustafa

May the book and HOLT's global database help you achieve your value creation goals.

Bartley J Madden

Hardcover: 978-0-9885969-5-5
Paperback: 978-0-9885969-6-2
ebook: 978-0-9885969-7-9

Published by LearningWhatWorks, Naperville, Illinois

Printed in the United State of America

Interior Design: Vicky Vaughn Shea, PonderosaPineDesign.com
Cover Design: Kit Foster, KitFosterDesign.com
Copyeditor: Mark Woodworth, Editmarks.weebly.com
Publishing Strategist: Holly Brady, HollyBrady.com

TABLE OF CONTENTS

PART II: A KNOWLEDGE-BUILDING CULTURE IS CRITICAL TO A FIRM'S LONG-TERM SURVIVAL AND SUCCESS

PART III: THE FIRM'S PERFORMANCE AND VALUATION

In celebration of my wife, Maricela,
and children, Gregory, Jeffrey, Miranda, and Lucinda

Praise for *Value Creation Thinking*

"In a world where short-term thinking has taken hold for too many managers and investors, *Value Creation Thinking* provides a much-needed perspective on the key drivers of long-term value.

Madden unites the fundamentals of financial valuation with a unique emphasis on corporate purpose, culture, and knowledge. Based on decades of research and practice, *Value Creation Thinking* sheds light on enduring sources of competitive advantage and exposes how traditional business thinking and accounting practices often distract managers and investors from sustained performance.

By speaking the language of both shareholders and stakeholders, Madden provides an important contribution to our understanding of capitalism at a critical moment and an illuminating roadmap for the future of business."

— Dominic Barton, Global Managing Director, McKinsey & Co.

"Bart Madden has written a provocative book that seeks to gain legitimacy for capitalism as the best way to mobilize society's scarce resources in order to advance human progress. He understands that the opposite of innovation is stagnation, not stability. The book provides clear guidance to embattled CEOs and directors seeking to pilot their firms through the chaotic market conditions of today's globally-connected business world. Madden's proposed Life-Cycle Reviews offer a means for CEOs and directors to improve their capital expenditure decisions and counteract Wall Street's excessive focus on quarterly earnings.

The book should be used in business schools to enable students to better understand the purpose of the firm and management's related responsibilities. Business students and many others will appreciate the insights from life-cycle thinking that connect long-term corporate performance to stock prices.

Madden notes that we should all want free-market capitalism to triumph over crony capitalism, which uses the coercive power of government to stifle competition. His approach is to deeply examine how firms can nurture a knowledge-building culture, innovate, and create long-term value. In my work, I focus on how managements can communicate their firms' and capitalism's dynamic contributions to the broader society. My work challenges CEOs and directors to engage with the political world in defense of capitalism. These two approaches are very different, and yet complementary."

— **Fred L. Smith, founder of the Competitive Enterprise Institute and Director of CEI's Center for Advancing Capitalism**

"A free society is an engine of wealth creation because individuals are free to pursue low-cost means of satisfying customer wants, and to innovate new methods and new products. Bart Madden's *Value Creation Thinking* is driven by the philosophy that an understanding of that process defines a path to the long-term increase in investor returns. Principles abound—life cycle modeling of firm dynamics, system thinking, and the management priorities of CEOs from Charles Koch to John Allison and John Mackey. We learn why firms like Eastman Kodak failed and why major product innovations like Michelin's run-flat tires failed. A firm's culture is shown to play an exceedingly important role in delivering value to customers and achieving long-run profitability. Beware the crony capitalist firm seeking profits from favors; the money is in creating value for customers."

— **Vernon L. Smith, Professor of Economics, Finance and Law**
Chapman University
Noble Laureate in Economics, 2002

"This book is simply outstanding and a must-read for any CEO or business leader who wants to manage their business in a way that creates and grows true, sustainable value. It clearly shows how to view and manage a company as a value creation system, how to use the three fundamental measures of value creation, and how to incorporate this "worldview" into the company's decision-making process. Madden presents a rich and insightful framework concerning the way mission, values, and purpose must be crafted to engage the company's workforce in the drive to create value. The book delves into how engendering a knowledge-building culture within a company drives value. Finally, it drives home the critical importance of culture—how it forms, and how it directly improves performance. This is the first book I have come across that ties all of these fundamental concepts together—value creation, value measures, company purpose, worldview, and culture in such an understandable and useful way. I will have my management team not only read *Value Creation Thinking*, but live by it. Again, a must-read!"

— **J. Thomas Gruenwald, Chief Executive Officer,
Westell Technologies**

PREFACE

The ideas in this book reflect how my worldview evolved. That is, our life experiences shape the lens (worldview) through which we interpret and interact with the world. My worldview is the result of a long intellectual journey that focused on three broad research areas. First, I developed an understanding of how the world works from a bottom-up, company-specific perspective, which led to the development of the life-cycle valuation framework—the centerpiece of this book. Second, beginning in the early 1980s, I worked in earnest to better understand how we know what we think we know and how this applies to problem solving. That work is summarized in my book *Reconstructing Your Worldview: The Four Core Beliefs You Need to Solve Complex Business Problems* and impacted my views on a knowledge-building culture—a frequent topic in this book. Third is the application of systems thinking and free-market principles to public policy, especially health care. That resulted in my 2012 book *Free to Choose Medicine: Better Drugs Sooner at Lower Cost* (see freetochoosemedicine.com).

Since the life-cycle valuation framework plays such a central role in this book, here is some relevant history. In 1969, Charles G. Callard and I cofounded Callard, Madden & Associates (CMA) and began a research program to better understand levels and changes in stock prices worldwide in order to improve investment decision making. In the early years, my focus was on a "model corporation" project (see Chapter 7). It was used to develop the complete life-cycle valuation model, including the translation of accounting data into economic returns, which resulted in the CFROI (cash-flow-return-on-investment) metric. Callard focused on macroeconomic forecasts and the economic reasons for changes in the market-implied discount rate; i.e., nominal tax rates for interest, dividends, and capital gains, plus inflation. My subsequent 1999 book, *CFROI Valuation: A Total System Approach to Valuing the Firm,* summarized most of this early work. The insights and data about discount rates presented in that book were based on Callard's original discount rate research.

I spent many years at CMA working with Bob Hendricks on consulting assignments to assist corporate managements with strategic decisions attuned to value creation. In 1984, I left CMA to manage money and continued my research on the life-cycle framework. Shortly thereafter, four CMA principals—Bob Hendricks, Eric Olsen, Marvin Lipson, and Rawley Thomas—founded HOLT Planning Associates to commercialize the life-cycle valuation framework for both money management and corporate organizations. The corporate advisory part of HOLT Planning Associates was acquired by the Boston Consulting Group in 1992 and the remaining money management advisory business was renamed HOLT Value Associates and led by Hendricks. I joined HOLT Value Associates in 1993 and enjoyed being part of a team that continued the research program and expanded the global database. In 2000, HOLT spun out a money management unit, Ironbridge Capital Management, headed by Chris Faber.

HOLT Value Associates was acquired by Credit Suisse in 2002 and the new business unit was managed by Tim Bixler, formerly a partner at HOLT. I retired from Credit Suisse as a Managing Director in 2003. Since then, I have been doing independent research, writing articles and books, plus presenting my ideas to business students. In particular, presentations to MBA students at DePaul University sharpened some of the ideas in this book. These presentations were coordinated through DePaul's Center for Strategy, Execution, and Valuation, directed by Professor Mark Frigo.

Today, Credit Suisse HOLT's database covers 20,000 companies from

67 countries and is used by 800 of the world's largest money management organizations. Key firm performance measurements, including CFROIs from the HOLT database, are currently used to produce the annual *Barron's 500* company ranking and *Forbes Ranking of the World's Most Innovative Companies.*

Over the years, significant research contributions were made by Rawley Thomas, Sam Eddins, and Tom Hillman (who is Managing Director and Global Head of HOLT Valuation & Analytics), Ron Graziano, and Mike McConnell. David Holland and Bryant Matthews are coauthors of the forthcoming book *Beyond Earnings,* which updates my *CFROI Valuation* book. Jim Ostry and Michel Lerner are Managing Directors and coleaders of Credit Suisse HOLT and, among other responsibilities, orchestrate feedback from money manager clients that helps advance ongoing research. Rick Faery is Managing Director of HOLT Corporate Advisory, which is focused on corporate applications of the life-cycle valuation framework and the HOLT global database.

Most of the above people have read draft versions of this book and provided helpful comments and criticisms. In addition, I benefitted from suggestions made by the following: Joe Cursio, Amit Dugar, Lee Hayes, Keith Howe, Shepherd Pryor, and Mark Ubelhart. My long-time editor and a former journalism professor, Marie Murray, improved the language, and in some cases the logic, throughout the book. Holly Brady did a superb job orchestrating the production of this book, which contains a considerable number of figures expertly crafted by Kimberly Allgaeuer.

Here is a brief overview of the key ideas, by chapter. Chapter 1 focuses on the public's declining trust in capitalism due to a series of high-profile events, including the complex financial products that temporarily boosted profits for the financial industry but soon fueled the 2007/2008 financial crisis. A distinction is made between the crony capitalism that is now on the rise in America and genuine free-market capitalism. The potential role of CEOs in defending free-market capitalism is illustrated in the pro–free-market management approaches of John Allison, T. J. Rodgers, and John Mackey.

Chapter 2 introduces the life-cycle principles that put a spotlight on how managerial skill and competition play out over time. The life-cycle framework is exceedingly useful for understanding firms' long-term track records. The ability to gain insights from studying history is a powerful skill now in widespread use by institutional money managers.

The ongoing debate about 21st century capitalism, income inequality, short-termism (typified by management's hyperfocus on meeting or exceeding Wall Street's quarterly expectations), various shareholder versus stakeholder controversies, and much more would all benefit from clarity about a firm's purpose and its management's core responsibilities (covered in Chapter 3). One conclusion is that maximizing shareholder value is best viewed as a result of achieving the firm's purpose.

Chapter 4 expands on one of management's responsibilities, which is to sustain a knowledge-building culture focused on innovation. Attention is given to improving one's worldview in order to more efficiently pinpoint obsolete assumptions and improve one's knowledge base. Chapter 4 borrows heavily from my 2012 article "Management's Worldview: Four Critical Points about Reality, Language, and Knowledge Building to Improve Organization Performance," which was published in the *Journal of Organizational Computing and Electronic Commerce*.

Culture is analyzed in Chapter 5, including the differences between a high-performance culture and a dysfunctional one. How cultures affect organizational performance is discussed for Toyota, the Cleveland Clinic, and Koch Industries.

Throughout the book, long-term, life-cycle track records for firms are displayed and analyzed in order to plainly show how business firms create or dissipate value. Chapter 6 connects the life-cycle variables—economic returns, reinvestment rates, and their fade rates over time—to market valuations. The life-cycle valuation model is shown to have unique advantages over other valuation approaches, and these advantages apply equally to management as well as investors. The case study of Walmart explains exactly what drives excess returns in the stock market.

Chapter 7 covers technical issues for those readers who are well versed in finance/valuation. One key idea is that the valuation of firms should be a continual learning process. This chapter highlights the thinking behind the development of the CFROI (cash-flow-return-on-investment) metric for use in the life-cycle valuation model.

Chapter 8 discusses important, yet subtle, issues about high-performing firms, including the halo effect that leads to erroneous conclusions about the causes of firm performance yet is remarkably widespread in popular business books. The role of experimentation is contrasted via the track records of JCPenney and Intuit. A case is made that how employees (especially management) *think* can become a source of unique competitive advantage.

Finally, because I favor using visuals to communicate ideas, I present a great many figures throughout this book. To coincide with publication of the book, I plan to post a slide deck, titled "Value Creation Thinking," on the website ValueCreationThinking.com. It will contain most of the figures in the book plus key points from various chapters. In the future, I'll post on this website links to YouTube videos of presentations that I make covering material in the book. Currently, Chapter 4 is summarized in a YouTube video, called "Reconstructing Your Worldview in Five Minutes." This material should help promote discussion of the ideas in the book, especially in classrooms.

PART I:
ECONOMIC PROGRESS AND MANAGEMENT'S CORE RESPONSIBILITIES

CHAPTER 1
Capitalism and Economic Progress

This is what we know to be true: business is good because it creates value, it is ethical because it is based on voluntary exchange, it is noble because it can elevate our existence, and it is heroic because it lifts people out of poverty and creates prosperity. Free-enterprise capitalism is one of the most powerful ideas we humans have ever had.

—John Mackey and Raj Sisodia[1]

A society that puts equality before freedom will get neither. A society that puts freedom before equality will get a high degree of both.

—Milton Friedman[2]

Increasingly, the public has been losing trust in the capitalist system in which big corporations play the central role. The decline in trust stems from our all too vivid memories about high-profile events such as: the unethical behavior that led to Enron-type bankruptcies; big bank bailouts that removed penalties for high-risk behavior; "innovative" financial products that played a role in the 2007/2008 financial crisis and were designed to boost short-term profits for financial firms without providing genuine value to customers; instances of executive compensation disconnected from firm performance; a never-ending bull market for lobbyists who exert a heavy influence in the crafting of highly complex legislation, typically followed by even more complex regulations, as well as many unintended consequences; and the list goes on. For many, it is all too easy to lose sight of the primary benefit to society from business firms, which is the value to customers who use their products and services.

While America is losing trust in capitalism, cronyism (think how business is being done in Italy and Greece) is on the rise. Cronyism removes a level competitive playing field and puts a premium, not on efficiency and innovation, but on lobbying skill in Washington to seek special treatment. While it is easy to agree with this statement, it is not so easy for CEOs to put a stake in the ground in support of free-market principles and then curtail all their firms' lobbying activities. Start with the typical board of directors that will almost certainly insist that such actions will benefit the firms' competitors to the detriment of their own shareholders. This issue is not insurmountable, as seen in a later section of this chapter that describes three successful CEOs who *do* carry the torch for free-market capitalism.

The cronyism dilemma strongly suggests that *all the major participants* in our complex socioeconomic system need to better understand how value is created and shared as well as the process by which free-market capitalism—not crony capitalism—enables everyone to rise as high as their skills and determination can take them. But first, let's take a look at how culture plays such an important role in how the economic world works. The importance of culture can be observed both from a top-down macroeconomic perspective as well as a bottom-up business firm perspective.

A culture of dynamism

Capitalism and corporations are intimately involved. Public corporations provide: the pooling of capital, the spreading of risk, tradable shares for liquidity, limited liability for investors, and the creation and transmission of knowledge. In the United States, this all began with the railroads' use of the joint stock, limited liability form of organization. The result was a long-term boost to society's dynamism as well as a surge in the creation of wealth, which greatly improved the living standard of almost everyone.

A remarkable example of a wealth creator was Henry Ford who, through revolutionary gains in manufacturing efficiency, changed automobile ownership from being a luxury item only available to the rich into an affordable product for most people. Ford's Model T made horse-drawn carriages obsolete and, for city dwellers, eliminated a huge health problem caused by breathing in pulverized manure from the large number of horses on city streets.

Note in this one example the significance of a new idea that improved on (and obsoleted) a status quo way of providing value to customers. This tells us that economic *growth,* absent big innovation, may very well *not* improve our standard of living in a meaningful way. How much better off would city dwellers have been if the horse population and horse-drawn carriages (components of capital stock of the time) had grown at, say, the typical 3 percent per year? Growth would have been achieved and more horse-drawn transportation provided, but not the type of growth possible through big innovations such as the Model T. These kind of innovations are emblematic of the goal of capitalism, which is the development of better solutions to human problems and making those solutions widely available.[3] Ford's Model T greatly improved existing means of ground transportation and, in turn, created opportunities for new auto-related businesses. Later, the automotive internal combustion engine was improved and adapted to provide power for airplanes. That innovation then solved the problem of long-distance transportation, while also creating widespread opportunities for ever more travel-related businesses. And so it goes.

To be sure, every new idea does not automatically solve a problem or easily scale up to widespread use. The functional elegance of capitalism resides in experiments, failures, learning, and the continual movement of resources to weed out bad ideas and advance good ones. This is a *bottom-up process* whereby individual firms compete to innovate in ways that can more efficiently deliver value to customers. Continual change and frequent business failure is the hallmark of a viable capitalist society.

In a society that embraces wealth creation, institutions facilitate collaboration and coordination. In addition, consumers need to be both willing and enthusiastic about trying new products and services. Institutions basically represent rules that shape acceptable behavior and thereby help or hinder economic progress. The rules are reflected in the maintenance of property rights, the workings of a nation's banking system, capital markets to fund new investments, laws to enable voluntary transactions, audited financial statements, and much more. There is no better way to create poverty than through the lack of wealth-facilitating institutions. Hernando de Soto makes a strong argument that the absence of property rights is a driving force for world poverty. He explains how undocumented houses, businesses, and the like in poor countries result in an inability to prove ownership, and consequently this amounts to "dead" capital that is unavailable for use in productive ways.[4]

In his book *Mass Flourishing: How Grassroots Innovation Created Jobs, Challenge, and Change,* the Nobel Prize–winning economist Edmund Phelps argues that economic progress is the result of *dynamism*: that is, a culture of experimentation, exploration, collaboration, and imagination.

A person's flourishing comes from the experience of the new: new situations, new problems, new insights, and new ideas to develop and share. Similarly, prosperity on a national scale—mass flourishing—comes from broad involvement of people in the process of innovation: the conception, development, and spread of new methods and products—indigenous innovation down to the grassroots.[5]

Phelps recognizes that our attitudes and beliefs are of the utmost importance in achieving economic progress. For society's members to conclude that capitalism merits their support, they need to experience that rewards go to those who work hard and work smart to deliver value to customers.[6] A key point is that it is easier to observe wealth creation through dynamism at the level of individual firms. So, throughout this book are examples of how managements orchestrate knowledge-building cultures that yield efficiency gains and innovations that, over the long haul, benefit all the firms' stakeholders. These straightforward, factual stories about value creation (and also dissipation) add a needed dimension to the often-heard abstract debates about how society should best be organized.

When the unit of analysis is an individual firm, there is no ambiguity about gains or losses in market valuations, the extent of value delivered to customers, and employment gains or losses. But when the unit of analysis is the macroeconomy, measurements become less refined. Nevertheless, Phelps and other economists have studied long historical periods and make a strong case that a culture of dynamism, with its emphasis on consumer choice and competition (i.e., capitalism), is the best path forward.[7] From a systems perspective, the spirit of dynamism is seen ideally in continual innovations, the willingness of consumers to try new things, and the enthusiasm of people to collaborate and bring needed skills to startup businesses, as well as in laws and regulations that benefit society while simultaneously facilitating change (as opposed to increasing complexity that imposes chokeholds on experimentation and entrepreneurship).

The next section offers very condensed looks at three CEOs who have a *deep understanding of the socioeconomic system in which their firms operate.* One CEO, John Allison, is now retired after a long tenure, while T. J. Rodgers and John Mackey founded their firms and are on their way to exceptionally long tenure in their leadership roles. These CEOs' strong belief in free-market principles became the basis for their firms' cultures, and they have all been proactive in explaining their beliefs in their speeches, Congressional testimonies, op-ed articles, and books.

CEOs carrying a torch for free-market capitalism

John Allison

In 1989, John Allison became CEO of BB&T, currently the tenth largest bank/financial services firm in the U.S. During his 20-year tenure as CEO, assets grew from $4.5 billion to $152 billion. BB&T produced solid shareholder returns and, remarkably, reported no quarterly losses during the 2007/2008 financial crisis while many of its competitors were headed toward bankruptcy or government bailouts. The firm's intense focus on customers and employees was reflected in the highest client satisfaction and lowest employee turnover rates relative to its banking peers. BB&T, under Allison's leadership, demonstrates that customers, employees, and shareholders have mutual long-term interests—a recurrent theme of this book.

By way of background, Allison has spent much time studying philosophy as well as economics. He is a passionate and articulate defender of capitalism on both economic and moral grounds and is a libertarian.[8] After BB&T, Allison was CEO from 2012 to 2015 at CATO, the well-known libertarian think tank.

BB&T, under Allison's leadership, is an excellent model of how to fulfill the core responsibilities of management that are recommended in this book (see Chapter 3). Particularly important are the nurturing and sustaining of a knowledge-building culture (Chapters 4 and 5). In his books and interviews, Allison explains how a business needs a well-defined purpose (vision), which for BB&T was to create the best financial institution possible. The mission statement, as shown on the company's website, follows:

- Helping our clients achieve economic success and financial security;

- Creating a place where our associates can learn, grow, and be fulfilled in their work;
- Making the communities in which we work better places to be; and thereby
- Optimizing the long-term return to our shareholders, while providing a safe and sound investment.

Allison views leadership as facilitating a process whereby beliefs influence the behavior that subsequently produces results. For employees to continue working and being successful at BB&T, they have to deeply understand the firm's beliefs (documented on the firm's website, titled "The BB&T Philosophy"). Employees need to actually live the beliefs in their daily work activities. In so doing, they have a cultural compass that provides a solid moral foundation for making their business decisions. Considerable effort is put into employee training focused on beliefs and behavior, including critical thinking skills, in order to minimize deep-seated emotional biases. To no one's surprise, BB&T's decentralized organizational structure gives its highly trained employees considerably more freedom to deal with clients, compared to other large banks.

Two particular examples of BB&T's culture reveal much. After the U.S. Supreme Court upheld a municipality's right to use eminent domain to seize a citizen's property to facilitate economic development, BB&T issued a statement that it would not make loans for any projects related to land seized by the government. Allison explained his decision as follows:

> In a certain sense this was both a hard decision and an easy decision, which our board unanimously endorsed. It was a hard decision in that we were worried about the economic consequences, in that we do business with a lot of municipalities that use eminent domain, and we knew that some of them would move their business from BB&T because of

our decision. On the other hand, given our whole value system and given the purpose we have in our organization, we simply could not in good conscience finance one individual using the government—the power of a gun—to take property from another individual. We couldn't finance a big box retailer throwing some poor little old lady out who didn't want to sell her home. If she wanted to sell it, fine. But the government taking your home is inconsistent with a free society, it's inconsistent with the principles that underlie property rights, and it's inconsistent with BB&T's belief system. I couldn't look my employees in the eye and tell them that we were going to do that.[9]

The second example involved the 2007/2008 financial crisis. Leading up to the crisis, one way that banks and mortgage lenders were boosting short-term profits was by issuing *negative amortization* loans. This type of loan's monthly payments are less than the interest expense. Home buyers used these loans to purchase more expensive homes than they normally could afford. Their expectations were for a continuation of the bull market in home prices and an opportunity to refinance in the future with their home presumably being worth considerably more than the initial purchase price. BB&T bankers recommended that top management not sell these kind of loans, fearing that clients did not appreciate the all-too-real downside risk involved.

BB&T refused to sell negative amortization loans. Allison put it this way: "We have a moral obligation to help you be successful and I expect to make a profit doing it ... but I'm never going to make a decision that I consciously think is bad for my clients ... even if I can make a profit in the short term, because it will always come back to haunt me." When the subsequent sharp decline in home prices occurred, many buyers of negative amortization loans lost their homes and suffered severe financial problems.

T. J. Rodgers

While earning a PhD in electrical engineering from Stanford University, T. J. Rodgers invented and patented VMOS technology, which he then sold to American Microsystems. He went on to found Cypress Semiconductor in the early 1980s and has been the CEO ever since. Cypress is an innovative global leader in microcontrollers and specialized memories for embedded systems in a wide variety of products, including automotive, industrial, mobile devices, and such.

Rodgers is extremely outspoken and articulate about both the benefits of free-market capitalism and the need to minimize cronyism in government policies. On his firm's website is a link, "Philosophy of Business and Government." It archives his op-eds, videos, and testimonies, which reveal a keen mind and a passion for capitalism, purged of cronyism. For example, in his March 25, 1993, Congressional testimony he said:

> … Cypress makes data-communication chips used in electronic superhighways, memory chips for supercomputers, and microprocessor modules for massively parallel computers. We would benefit greatly if billions of taxpayer dollars were showered on the various technology projects favored by the Clinton administration. It would be easy for me to support these projects. I could spend one minute talking about our products, a few more discussing the wonders of the basic technologies, a few more minutes on the serious peril we face from other countries, especially the government-financed Japanese and Europeans, and finally, I could ask for a dole—to save American high technology.
>
> But I am here to say that such subsidies will hurt my company and our industry. Why? Because they represent tax-and-spend economics—a brand of economics that is a known failure. I do not want handouts. The men and

women of our company do not want handouts. And if Congress wants to help American high technology, handouts are the wrong way to go—especially if they are funded with huge tax increases on individuals and corporations.[10]

Based on his track record of innovation, one could easily label T. J. Rodgers an entrepreneur. But entrepreneurs are typically associated with startup businesses, not CEOs of large, successful companies. A more accurate description would be to say he is a *wealth creator.* This is a more precise use of language because it encourages our thinking about relationships and the complex interdependencies involved with the process of how wealth is created. Wealth creators may be called inventors, entrepreneurs, innovators, managers, or whatever, yet they fundamentally succeed by "thinking smart" in order to solve problems, seize opportunities, collaborate, and motivate people. And they *commercialize* new ideas, as opposed to simply getting patents on inventions that never scale up to deliver value to a significant number of customers.

Within Cypress, Rodgers has successfully orchestrated a series of autonomous businesses, with the parent company acting as venture capitalist for the funding. One notable Cypress success is SunPower, which today is one of the largest solar energy companies and widely acknowledged as the technology leader in delivering the highest efficiency solar cells. In the early 2000s, researchers at SunPower had developed superlative technology to produce very high efficiency solar cells but were running out of money and lacked the necessary managerial skill to create a viable business. Rogers orchestrated a capital infusion as well as the installation of Cypress's management processes at SunPower. Importantly, he transferred key Cypress managers to SunPower. The original investment of $143 million resulted in a total of $3.2 billion being distributed to Cypress shareholders. This type of bottom-up business innovation, coupled to consumers willing to try new technology, is a prime example of the type of dynamism that Edmund Phelps argues is so important to economic progress.

T. J. Rodgers' managerial skill and passion for innovation, combined with the resources from the company he founded, enabled SunPower to survive and eventually lead the solar revolution. That is of the utmost importance to environmentalists and many others concerned with providing clean electric power. Free-market capitalism is an extraordinarily efficient way for society to solve problems and use resources wisely, and, in so doing, make the world a better place.

John Mackey

John Mackey cofounded Whole Foods Market in 1980. As Co-CEO he has been instrumental in building the firm into the leading provider of natural and organic foods while instilling a wealth-creation culture focused on win–win relationships in all aspects of this business. Before starting Whole Foods, he described himself as a person with long hair and a long beard who lived in communal housing. His political views were on the left, and he viewed corporations as evil because they selfishly sought only profits. After three decades of managing Whole Foods, his view has changed:

> Becoming an entrepreneur and starting a business completely changed my life. Almost everything I had believed about business was proven to be wrong. The most important thing I learned in my first year … was that business isn't based on exploitation or coercion at all. Instead, I discovered that business is based on cooperation and voluntary exchange. People trade voluntarily for mutual gain. No one is forced to trade with a business. Customers have competitive alternatives in the marketplace, team members have competitive alternatives for their labor, investors have

numerous alternatives to invest their capital, and suppliers have plenty of alternative customers for their products and services. Investors, labor, management, suppliers—they all need to cooperate to create value for customers. If they do, the joint value created is divided fairly among the creators of the value through competitive market processes based approximately on the overall contribution each stakeholder makes. In other words, business is not a zero sum game with a winner and a loser. It is a win, win, win, win game— and I really like that.[11]

Although Whole Foods has a very small share of the U.S. supermarket food industry, it has been an important stimulus for healthier eating. Today, the firm faces an accelerating trend in new competition which, in the future, may well lower its historic return on capital and asset growth rate.

Mackey is well known for his passionate belief that business must simultaneously pursue profits as well as a higher purpose, while creating a harmony of interests among the firm's mutually dependent stakeholders. In their book *Conscious Capitalism,* Mackey and Raj Sisodia, a professor of marketing at Bentley University, point out key differences between a worldview that focuses in the extreme on corporate social responsibility (CSR) versus their own pro-capitalism worldview. Specifically, the former worldview considers CSR as independent of the firm's purpose and an ethical add-on to business goals. Whereas for the latter worldview, according to Mackey and Sisodia, CSR is *embedded* in the firm through its higher purpose and concern for all stakeholders.

Is capitalism a moral system?

Who has not heard that capitalism is an uncaring system, or is rooted in greed, or lacks a sound moral foundation? These often-heard criticisms are mistaken perceptions implying that supporters of capitalism are uncaring about other people. At many levels of analysis, this is wrong.

An understanding of how market-based capitalism actually works leads to a transition from greed to self-interest. Transactions in the market improve one's position or else they would not voluntarily occur. Further reflection reveals that voluntary transactions in organized markets (trade/globalization) help a wide diversity of others whom one does not know personally. This is crucial assistance to enable people to pull themselves out of poverty. In fact, if not for specialization that empowers comparative advantage, coupled to organized impersonal markets, we would all be in poverty. Instead of ready access to continually improving transportation, communication, food, medicine, and more, we would have been living short, dreary, and disheartening lives.

Capitalism may appear to be focused in the extreme on meeting material needs and in creating new wants. But, fundamentally, it is all about discovery and new opportunities that truly broaden the range of human possibility. Capitalism is the best way to break the iron grip of a dysfunctional society that spawns poverty and eliminates the birth of new opportunities. Capitalism trades war and mutual loss for markets and mutual gain.

Whereas trade in small groups relies on shared cultural norms and reciprocity, impersonal markets in which you do not have a personal relationship with your trading partner dominate our economic lives. Impersonal markets require adequate institutional rules of behavior in order to function properly. In addition, for a capitalistic society to endure, the public needs to *trust that the system for determining financial success or failure is fair.* The public does not easily forget the sky-high compensation paid to CEOs that subsequently sent their firms to bankruptcy court or hat in hand to the government. Examples include Global Crossing, Enron, and Tyco in the early 2000s, and bailouts to large financial firms in the 2007/2008 financial crisis.

People sense something is very wrong when financial firms can profit in the short term but get bailed out by the government when they subsequently lose their highly levered bets. Heads I win, tails I get bailed out.

We need government to deliver smart laws and regulations that create a level, competitive playing field. Yet, in practice, laws and regulations continue to directly favor large organizations with big lobbying budgets and the politically connected with subsidies, exemptions, and assorted tax breaks and, more indirectly, with barriers that eliminate potential competitors that are ill-equipped to handle the complex regulatory load imposed on specific industries.

When a big percentage of the public concludes that the system favors the rich and powerful to the detriment of everyone else, expect big political change. Regrettably, we are headed in a direction in which change will most likely not embrace a better free-market infrastructure. Unless we alter direction, we can expect even more complex laws and regulations, imposing a top-down "solution" to a problem that needs less cronyism and more bottom-up, free-market dynamism.

Capitalism that truly provides a level competitive playing field without cronyism is increasingly being called *free-market capitalism*. That the U.S. is sliding down a slippery slope away from free-market capitalism is neatly summarized by Raghuram G. Rajan and Luigi Zingales, professors at the University of Chicago:

> We do think that capitalism—or more precisely, the free enterprise system—in its ideal form is the best system to allocate resources and rewards. But the forms of capitalism that are experienced in most countries are very far from the ideal. They are a corrupted version in which vested interests prevent competition from playing its natural, healthy role. Many of the accusations against capitalism—that it oppresses workers, creates private monopolies, and allows

only the rich to get richer—apply not to a true free enterprise system but rather to the corrupt, uncompetitive versions that we observe around the world.

... Capitalism's biggest political enemies are not the fire-
brand trade unionists spewing vitriol against the system but
the executives in pin-striped suits who extol the virtues of
competitive markets with every breath while attempting to
extinguish them with every action.[12]

Management plays a uniquely important role in the ongoing debate
about 21st century capitalism. To achieve real progress in this debate, we
should start with a clear understanding about the purpose of the firm and
management's core responsibilities. A case is made here that management
needs to get actively engaged with the defense of free-market capitalism
that enables firms to prosper while benefitting customers, employees,
shareholders, and other stakeholders alike.

CHAPTER 2

The Firms' Competitive Life Cycle

There is no more important proposition in economic theory than that, under competition, the rate of return on investment tends towards equality in all industries. Entrepreneurs will seek to leave relatively unprofitable industries and enter relatively profitable industries.

—George Stigler[13]

A surprising number of innovations fail not because of some fatal technological flaw or because the market isn't ready. They fail because responsibility to build these businesses is given to managers or organizations whose capabilities aren't up to the task.... Most often the very skills that propel an organization to succeed in sustaining circumstances systematically bungle the best ideas for disruptive growth. An organization's capabilities become its disabilities *when disruptive innovation is afoot.*

—Clayton M. Christensen and Stephen P. Kaufman[14]

Foundational principles

What the Nobel laureate economist George Stigler is saying just above, is that in a *competitive* environment, and for a period of time, a firm's profitability can exceed the average rate. This is due to *managerial skill* and/or the production of a commodity with a constrained supply. But then, other firms have an incentive to duplicate the skill and/or invest to either expand the supply or produce an economically viable substitute. The reverse also holds. That is, sustained below-average profitability leads to contraction as capital seeks to achieve higher returns elsewhere. These principles explain a firm's performance over its "life cycle."

Competition is ever present. The process of competition driving a firm's return on its invested capital toward the cost of capital has been observed and studied for quite some time. It is the basis for the life-cycle valuation framework (explained below) that enables one to intuitively understand both a firm's financial performance over time as well as investor expectations that are embedded in current stock prices.

For example, just before the stock market crash of 1929, the well-known economist Irving Fischer made the famous remark "Stocks have reached what looks like a permanently high plateau." In sharp contrast, the investment analyst and author of *A Scientific Approach to Investment Management,* Dwight C. Rose, made a presentation, "Common Stocks at the Current Price Level," at the December 27, 1928, joint annual meeting of the American Statistical Association and the American Economic Association. He astutely noted:

> The average efficiency of business has increased. Those that
> do not keep up with the times must fall by the wayside in
> competition; those that are ahead of the times will show a
> correspondingly greater progress; but the *average* company
> will do little better than the average company has done in
> the past. In the last analysis we have a competition of capital

seeking investment in any enterprise offering more than the average return, and more capital will continue to pour into such enterprises until the return of the average concern is on a basis commensurate with that in other fields.[15]

Rose calculated that current stock prices for most firms embedded a forecast of returns on capital being sustained at levels greatly in excess of the average long-term return earned by the corporate sector. His conclusion: "… bidding for seasoned common stocks has inflated their market values to levels from which there must be a recession." In contrast to Irving Fischer, Dwight Rose had a sound economic logic for predicting the great stock market crash that began in 1929.

This particular bit of history is a useful reminder of how the life-cycle principles used by Rose are foundational to understanding stock prices. Knowledge about the life-cycle valuation framework leads to better corporate decisions concerned with major capital allocations and to a much needed source for empirical facts (i.e., firms' life-cycle track records) that are sorely lacking in debates about the future of capitalism and about the thorny issues concerning shareholders versus other stakeholders.

The life-cycle valuation framework

You can use this framework as a sound basis to construct historical track record charts that provide easy-to-understand insights about the connections between firms' financial performance and long-term levels and changes in stock prices. Instead of relying on earnings per share figures to gauge performance, *economic returns* (cash flow–based returns on investment) are calculated and displayed versus the *cost of capital* (investors' demanded returns). A firm's *reinvestment rates* (approximated by a firm's asset growth rates) are also plotted. *The rate at which economic returns fade over the long term toward the cost of capital is the most important forecast variable for knowledgeable investors who seek to earn excess investment returns in*

21

the stock market. The life-cycle explanation of how wealth is created or dissipated is especially useful for putting a spotlight on the false belief that management can increase shareholder value by "growing the business" regardless of whether economic returns are above or below the cost of capital. The life-cycle framework is an integral part of the investment process at a great many large institutional money management organizations, and is increasingly being utilized in the corporate world.

Figure 2.1 illustrates transitional stages in a stylized life-cycle history of a firm. Life-cycle charts, using actual company data, are displayed throughout this book.

Figure 2.1: The competitive life-cycle view of the firm

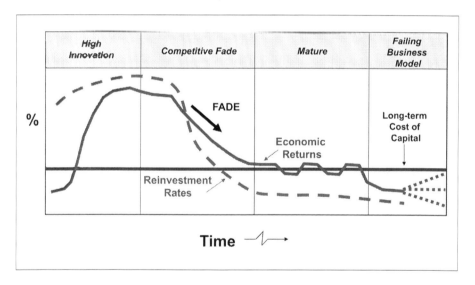

As a startup firm successfully commercializes new ideas that efficiently provide value to customers, a life-cycle chart would show economic returns increasing well above the cost of capital. In the *high-innovation* stage, high reinvestment rates indicate further success in scaling up the innovation and creating significant additional wealth. As noted earlier, a firm's demonstrated wealth creation success in earning well above-average (above the cost of capital) economic returns signals other firms that they should compete in hopes of earning above-cost-of-capital returns themselves. The combination of high economic returns and high reinvestment rates typically reflects that an opportunity is sizable. This is a magnet that attracts new competitors. Consequently, a firm eventually transitions into a *competitive fade* stage wherein economic returns fade toward the cost of capital and reinvestment rates also fade toward lower rates of growth.

As firms fade, they become larger enterprises and encounter managerial challenges about how to direct increasingly complex organizations. All the while, their competitors are working to better serve customers. The result of this process is that, over time, firms eventually earn approximately cost-of-capital economic returns and, due to their larger size and the new competition, their reinvestment rates tend to be close to an economy-type growth rate. Oftentimes, management and boards equate success with firm size and lose sight of the need to continually nurture opportunities to earn above the cost of capital. At the *mature* stage, firms may have a significant share of a product/service market, and this can lead to complacency and a business-as-usual mindset that focuses in the extreme on improving the efficiency of existing operations to the detriment of new opportunities. Moreover, a firm's organizational structure that has evolved to improve existing business processes can all too easily become rigid and be a significant deterrent to the development of innovative new business models.

A transition to the *failing business model* stage is typically observed in highly bureaucratic firms with a strong business-as-usual culture. Management's competitive shortfall might have been accelerated by outside innovators who have developed superior ways to meet customer needs and/or by industry competitors with more viable cultures that are better at continual, overall efficiency improvements. The task then is to purge business-as-usual practices, to restructure, and quite possibly to hire new management who are not wedded to the firm's past ways. Eventually, a firm either improves or enters bankruptcy. In the company example below, Eastman Kodak, a former blue chip company, eventually was forced into bankruptcy. The world had changed and Eastman Kodak was too slow to adapt.

In summary, Figure 2.1 is a stylized depiction of a firm's history that is useful for understanding the basic interplay of managerial skill and competition over time. Firms that have faded downward toward the average corporate return occasionally do surge up for a substantial number of years due to successful innovation (e.g., Apple). These situations tend to be unanticipated by investors and, as the higher corporate performance unfolds, market-beating shareholder returns are achieved.

Eastman Kodak's failure to adapt

Life-cycle charts have three panels each. The top panel displays economic returns calculated as a CFROI® (cash-flow-return-on-investment, a registered trademark of Credit Suisse Securities). CFROIs are inflation adjusted, sometimes referred to as *real* as opposed to *nominal*. They remove a variety of accounting distortions so the result is a more accurate readout of "true" economic returns than the conventional RONA (return-on-net-assets). Importantly, real CFROIs are directly comparable for levels and changes over long periods that include varying inflation rates (see Chapter 7 for more details). The top panel also displays the long-term corporate average CFROI as a dark horizontal line at 6 percent to approximate the real cost of capital.

The middle panel reflects a firm's reinvestment rate calculated as a real asset growth rate. The bottom panel indicates a firm's total shareholder return (dividends plus price appreciation) relative to the S&P 500 index. Out-performance is seen as a rising trend for the relative wealth line; market-matching performance is shown as a flat trend; and underperformance shows as a declining trend. Shareholder returns *above* or *below* the S&P 500 Index are driven by firms delivering life-cycle performance (economic returns and reinvestment rates) that *exceed* or *fall short* of investors' expectations at the beginning of the time period. The life-cycle data for Eastman Kodak in Figure 2.2 begins in 1960.

Figure 2.2: Eastman Kodak

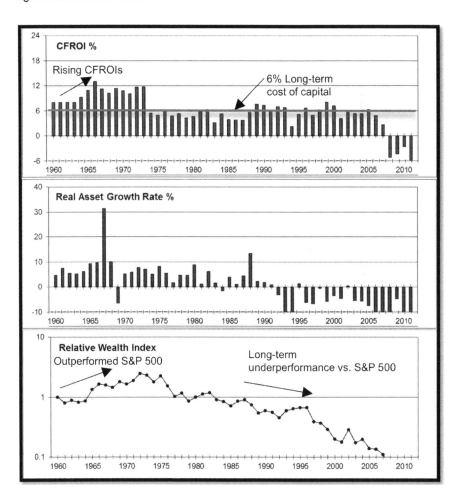

Source: Credit Suisse HOLT global database

A deep understanding of how best to meet customer needs is the beginning step of the wealth creation process. In the late 1800s, George Eastman, a wealth creator for sure, worked at a bank during the day and spent his evenings developing a way to overcome the technical headaches faced by professional photographers. His dry plate emulsion innovation clearly advanced the then-crude state of the art. Subsequently, he continually innovated and obsoleted his early work with a revolutionary camera designed to make photography available to everyone. His innovative camera had film inside, and he named it the "Kodak." Importantly, the Kodak camera was designed to be part of a customer-friendly system in which the customer sent the camera with its exposed film inside to Eastman's firm and then received back developed pictures and a fully reloaded camera. The Eastman Kodak value proposition was compelling, "You press the button, we do the rest."[16] This was quite similar in concept to the systems approach for purchasing and storing music used by Steve Jobs with the Apple iPod, which initially caught consumers' attention by offering "1,000 songs in your pocket." Owners of iPods press a button and Apple takes care of the rest.

Kodak dominated the film and camera market for decades, and then in the early 1960s introduced the Instamatic cartridge, which greatly simplified loading and unloading film. That innovation was the impetus for the surge in CFROIs to a 12 percent level by the mid-1970s (top panel of Figure 2.2). This rise in CFROIs was accomplished with significant real asset growth (middle panel). And this surge in economic performance was rewarded by a rising relative wealth line (bottom panel) as Kodak's stock price outpaced the S&P 500. Then, from its peak in the mid-1970s, Kodak's future was all downhill. What went wrong?

Kodak's core problem was a bloated and complacent bureaucratic culture that permeated all levels of the firm, thereby making any changes that were needed a very slow process indeed.[17] A series of CEOs was unable to address the issue of a slow-moving firm in what had become a new world of fast-paced change. With improved quality, Fuji film became a formidable competitor to Kodak's film. Worse, Kodak management still kept its resources focused on yesterday's technologies. Even though digital photography actually originated at Kodak, this hugely important innovation was ignored by management because it threatened the company's core film business. Although for a time Kodak did gain leadership in digital cameras, management then failed to anticipate the onslaught of cameras in cell phones and tablets. Also, they were late in seeing the impact of rapid consumer adoption of color printers in the home for reproducing photographs. As Kodak's march continued through the mature stage to the failing business stage, management pursued an endless stream of acquisitions, divestitures, and restructurings that led to massive layoffs and a demoralized workforce. Eventually, Kodak filed for bankruptcy in 2012. Later chapters discuss the knowledge-building cultures of Amazon and Intuit, which put their firms at the forefront of change—diametrically the opposite of Kodak's culture.

Why the life-cycle framework is so important

Without an intuitively understandable and operationally useful way to link a firm's financial performance to its stock prices, a treasure trove of *empirical facts* about how firms actually perform is unavailable to management. What is lost is the opportunity to learn by studying history. Historical analyses of company track records can be particularly useful for analyzing how management strategies play out over time. Another lost opportunity is at the public policy level, where an absence of historical perspective tends to result only in abstract arguments and acrimonious debates about the firm's role in society. It is far better for debates to be grounded in an economic reality reflected in histories of firms that show how essential it is to earn the cost of capital as a prerequisite to a firm's survival and long-term prosperity. It is one of the major goals of this book to describe the life-cycle framework that is so well suited to display relevant empirical facts in a straightforward manner.

It is a common belief that increasing quarterly earnings per share is always favorable for stock prices. This belief is wrong in many ways. For example, coupling financial leverage to below-cost-of-capital investments can increase earnings. Earnings can also rise by cutting back on research and development expenditures that are essential for long-term viability. Moreover, both academic studies and experience with calculations of investor expectations in stock prices strongly indicate that stock prices actually are a reflection of *long-term* forecasts of firms' financial performance.[18] A far better understanding of firms' stock prices is achieved with life-cycle variables instead of earnings. It is vitally important for management and boards alike to choose a workable valuation compass and not to be sidetracked by an excessive focus on quarterly earnings per share.

Why has there been such a widespread worldwide adoption of the life-cycle valuation framework by portfolio managers? Because it makes them smarter. Note that portfolio managers' compensation and job security is directly dependent on their analytical skill at:

- Understanding investor expectations implied in current stock prices
- Making insightful forecasts of plausible future scenarios within the context of firms' past performance
- Judging the impact of management's strategy and capital outlays in terms of how much wealth is likely to be created or dissipated

The life-cycle framework is ideally suited to these tasks. Note that these tasks are not just important to portfolio managers, but are equally important to management and board members.

Here is a summary of relevant guideposts using the life-cycle lens to analyze firms:

- For publicly traded firms at any stage of the life cycle, including early stage, it is worthwhile to track financial performance in life-cycle terms, then compare this to investor expectations in current stock prices. Managements of high-innovation stage firms in the startup phase need to quickly confirm or disconfirm the critical assumptions that fundamentally determine the viability of their business models.

- In the competitive-fade stage, *all else equal*, higher market valuations are accorded firms that are able to reinvest at high rates. But, all else is *not* equal, and higher reinvestment rates tend to result in faster fade of economic returns over time. This is due to accelerated competition responding to a big opportunity (signaled by high reinvestment rates) to create wealth, plus the added difficulty of managing a fast-growing firm. In addition, a huge influence on a firm's long-term fade is the degree of management's success in nurturing a knowledge-building culture. Such a culture has the potential to deliver stable processes and innovation with very favorable long-term fade, such as that exhibited by 3M (analyzed later in this chapter).

- Firms in the mature stage typically are burdened by considerable bureaucracy. For mature firms, it is especially important to continually improve the efficiency of their existing businesses while simultaneously developing new, wealth-creating innovations that have the potential to scale up to a significant size—*efficiency and innovation are the hallmarks of managerial skill*. Small, strategic acquisitions may help by providing new skills to leverage core competencies. However, merging with another large, mature company tends to make the problem of earning greater than cost of capital returns even more difficult to achieve.

- In the failing-business-model stage, one likely constraint to improvement is a management worldview that is strongly influenced by assumptions that are no longer valid. And such obsolete assumptions are most likely entrenched in the firm's culture. Getting back to earning the cost of capital, given this burden, may well require new management who have a different worldview and are more attuned to a changing business environment and able to successfully restructure the firm's operating assets and culture.

Life-cycle track records visually display how managements have dealt with changing environments. Did they assume that the future will mirror past success and remain steady at the wheel with business-as-usual practices? Or, did they actively seek feedback that informed them early on that a new direction was needed?

Changing environments and firm adaptability

An extraordinarily difficult challenge for management is to orchestrate continual improvement in the efficiency of today's operations while simultaneously building knowledge about evolving changes in the environment in order to innovate and adapt to do well in the future. An especially bad outcome occurs when managers' strongly held assumptions about the future being a continuation of a successful past results in a failure to recognize early signs of obsolescence.

This was clearly illustrated in the Eastman Kodak case when a young electronic engineer, Steve Sasson, who worked for Kodak, developed the first digital camera. Although Kodak did file a patent in 1976 for Sasson's invention, when he demonstrated it throughout the firm, management's reaction was ambivalent. That was but a reflection of Kodak's deep-seated culture of being a preeminent film company. The next two company examples illustrate managerial skill in orchestrating a knowledge-building culture that expertly did handle the two-part challenge of efficiency today, while simultaneously developing new innovative products for tomorrow.

3M's managerial skill

In the early 1900s, William McKnight joined 3M, then a struggling abrasives manufacturing company. He was fanatical about developing a deep understanding of customer problems, quality control, and innovation. The firm is a stellar example of a long-lived, knowledge-building culture that was started and nurtured by McKnight. He became president in 1929 and served as board chairman from 1949 to 1966. McKnight initiated the 3M policy of letting engineers spend up to 15 percent of their time pursuing new ideas of their own, which was—and is—more a symbol of freedom then a specific quantitative rule to be followed.[19]

At year-end 2014, 3M was a widely diversified manufacturing company with $32 billion in sales and 90,000 employees. The life-cycle chart in Figure 2.3 is remarkable in that wealth-creating economic returns (CFROIs) exceeding the cost of capital were maintained over the entire 1960 to 2014 time period.

Throughout its history, 3M employees have taken pride in their shared belief that innovation is the firm's lifeblood. The firm's culture nurtured the freedom to patiently experiment and collaborate. Innovations could begin with understanding customer needs or could be the result of a new discovery with no apparent, immediate commercial use. The latter innovations sometimes developed into technology platforms of considerable value to the firm.

However, 3M's free-spirited organizational culture resulted in costs spiraling upward and CFROIs declining by the late 1990s. In 2000, for the first time, the 3M board hired an outsider as CEO. James McNerney, a GE veteran and a strong advocate of Six Sigma process improvement, brought significant change to 3M. During his four-and-a-half-year tenure, CFROIs improved considerably as shown in the upper panel of Figure 2.3. This improved corporate performance, resulting in 3M's stock outperforming the market (lower panel of Figure 2.3) during McNerney's tenure as CEO. Nevertheless, some argue that while McNerney made tough, but necessary, cost-reduction decisions, the Six Sigma approach hurt the research labs' core innovation process. Achieving the best balance between efficiency and innovation is always a difficult challenge.[20]

Figure 2.3: 3M

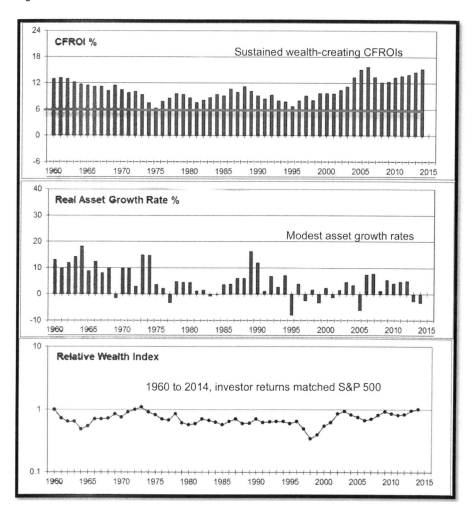

Source: *Credit Suisse HOLT global database*

Over the entire 1960 to 2014 time period, a 3M stockholder would have achieved a total shareholder return that approximated the S&P 500 total return (an overall basically flat line for relative wealth in the bottom panel of Figure 2.3). Why not higher? The answer is that throughout the period, investors priced the firm with *premium expectations (favorable forecast fade rates)*. The only truly significant multiyear surprise in corporate performance was during McNerney's tenure. Investors expected superior corporate performance, and the firm consistently delivered that kind of performance over the long haul. Invariably, investor returns approximate the market return when a firm's economic performance matches earlier investor expectations.

Keep in mind that many management books tout a rule about superior performance. That is, management should make many small bets, such as 3M has done. Yet context matters. For example, the exceptionally successful career of Elon Musk reflects a CEO who seized huge opportunities in electric cars (Tesla Motors) and low-cost reusable rockets (SpaceX) and solar panels (SolarCity)—huge bets for sure. Context matters a great deal.

Illumina and wealth creation

Recall the previous discussion on dynamism for spurring economic progress. Dynamism is about creativity, imagination, and new discoveries that can be put to practical use. It can involve an inventor or entrepreneur who develops an original idea with big potential, and it is also reflected in the collaboration and commercialization of ideas developed by others. This includes university research and strategic acquisitions. Illumina is a company that has been especially successful in both of these areas.

Illumina's 1999 through 2014 life-cycle chart, shown in Figure 2.4, represents a classic high-innovation-stage company that was unprofitable in its early years while it was gaining traction. But then, successful commercialization of its technology led to CFROIs surging to well above the cost of capital. Today, Illumina is by far the dominant firm for supplying the most technically advanced DNA sequencing machines. Sequencing a person's genome is the path forward for personalized medicine as well as the development of breakthrough new therapeutic treatments for humankind's worst diseases.

Figure 2.4: Illumina

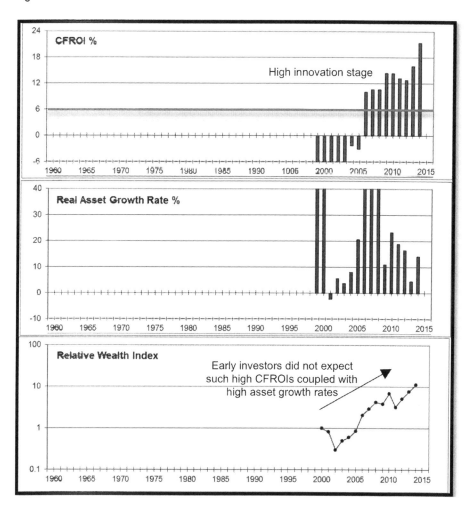

Source: Credit Suisse HOLT global database

The firm was started by licensing its technology from Tufts University. Illumina's success is widely attributed to the managerial skill of Jay Flatley, who became CEO in 1999. Early on, Flatley positioned Illumina to clearly beat a key competitor, Affymetrix. He believed that the competitive win over Affymetrix should be viewed as a stepping stone. Flatley's attention quickly shifted to rapid innovation in order to leapfrog ahead in the race to drop the cost of sequencing a person's DNA to under $1,000.

Flatley has a nose for acquiring breakthrough technology. In 2007, he made a huge strategic bet in acquiring Solexa. Illumina paid $600 million for Solexa, which at that time had zero revenues, but its technology was 100 times faster and 100 times cheaper than the existing technology for genome-sequencing. The resulting combination was extraordinarily effective in the marketplace. Illumina has made other smart strategic acquisitions and has expanded beyond sequencing technologies to services that produce genomic insights.

According to Flatley, Illumina's organizational culture has two especially significant features that make sense within the *context* of competing within a rapidly evolving technology revolution. First, he notes that all top-level managers have technology backgrounds; and second, the organization is structured to minimize bureaucracy in product development. According to Flatley:

> We think it's very important that the people who lead our company … have technology backgrounds…. To be the leader in this business, you can't just be a good general manager. We contrast it, for example, with a good GE general manager…. They believe their talent doesn't matter if they are managing a refrigerator factory or a locomotive factory. It's all about general management. We don't believe that, at least for our markets.
>
> One of the other really important things we did, early

on, was structured our product development process in a way where we could very efficiently run a large number of projects simultaneously. That is what has given us the ability to scale, in size and complexity and number of products, and still be able to manage with a limited number of top executives. That's because of how we empower our teams to go off and do great things. They only have to come back to us under a very fixed set of circumstances. We [in management] can set the strategy and direction and talk about specifications. They can do the execution, which they are really good at.[21]

Fundamentally, Illumina is both extraordinarily efficient as well as innovative in helping customers understand genetic variations that hold enormous potential for improvements in health.

The capitalist's dilemma

In their article "The Capitalist's Dilemma," Clayton Christensen (see the quote at the beginning of this chapter) and Derek van Bever, both of the Harvard Business School, make insightful observations about firms' resource allocation processes. They point out the need for *market-creating innovations* that drive costs down and enable products to reach big new segments of consumers (e.g., Ford's Model T) with their related job creation and new opportunities for other firms. However, an excessive focus on return-on-investment and financial spreadsheet analyses dampens management's appetite for the uncertainty and longer payoffs associated with market-creating innovations. Consequently, we observe a management mindset that often focuses on lower risk, *efficiency-improving innovations* to lower costs, and *performance-improving innovations* in new models. These do not do much for job creation.

These authors noted that Scott Cook, cofounder of Intuit (Chapter 8),

... has observed that a focus on financial outcomes too early in the innovation process produces a withering of ambition. He [Cook] argues that financial metrics lack predictive power. "Every one of our tragic and costly new business failures had a succession of great-looking financial spreadsheets," he says. Now new-product teams at Intuit do not submit a financial spreadsheet to begin work and testing; rather, he notes, they focus on "where we can change lives most profoundly."[22]

The capitalist's dilemma is that economic progress thrives on market-creating innovations. But that goes against short-term investment horizons held by those investors who typically view corporate performance solely in terms of quarterly earnings reports. The solution is for management and boards to better understand the wealth creation process and to realize that stock prices are, in fact, set by investors making what are actually long-term forecasts. In particular, an understanding of the life-cycle valuation framework puts the spotlight on *both* long-term levels and trends of economic returns as well as on reinvestment rates. The largest gains in market value come from firms that combine above-cost-of-capital economic returns along with high reinvestment rates. The exceptional gains in shareholder value for Amazon (Chapter 3) were primarily due to its extraordinarily high reinvestment rates (asset growth rates). This is all about market-creating innovations that require large capital outlays and patience. Another example is Walmart (Chapter 6), which outperformed the stock market 100-fold from 1970 to 1990 primarily due to a massive reinvestment of capital in scaling up its innovative business model with new store expansion. This type of large-scale wealth creation is about scaling up in a big way, which *necessitates hiring new employees* to do the additional work needed to deliver value to customers.

The key point is that the managerial challenge to both innovate and be efficient at the same time requires creativity on the part of management. And it requires that management not get side-tracked by accounting cost controls and early spreadsheet analyses that favor minor improvements while penalizing investment opportunities that have the potential to create new markets. An excessive focus on meeting the quarterly earnings expectations of short-term investors is a prime roadblock to taking a long-term view of building the business.

A first step in resolving the capitalist's dilemma is for management and board members to improve their knowledge about market valuation and to better understand how firms like Amazon have been so successful because they focus on long-term net cash receipts (often referred to as free cash flows) instead of short-term accounting earnings. Learn how long-term, life-cycle performance drives the *level* of a firm's market value and be less concerned about short-term *changes* in market value in reaction to quarterly results. To sum up, management should focus on creating long-term value and not be concerned with the "needs" of short-term investors.

CHAPTER 3

The Firm's Purpose and Management's Core Responsibilities

Businesses need to engage in institutional innovation—*innovation designed to shift the system, to reengineer the conditions that individual companies face.*

... At the most fundamental level, these companies and their leaders will operate from a mind-set of respect for the larger system that makes their own success and prosperity possible. They will consider it part of their job to ensure that their activities align with the effective functioning of the system and, at a minimum, do not undermine it. Some may call this social responsibility. We see it as enlightened self-interest.

... For anyone who believes as we do that the market system is the most powerful engine yet devised for generating wealth and improving living standards worldwide, what is important is that companies act in ways that ensure the system's ongoing health and sustainability.

—Joseph L. Bower, Herman B. Leonard, and Lynn S. Paine[23]

In my experience motivating employees with a sense of purpose is the only way to deliver innovative products, superior service and unsurpassed quality over the long haul.... An organization of highly motivated people is hard to duplicate. The motivation will last if it is deeply rooted in employees' commitment to the intrinsic purpose of their work.

—Bill George[24]

Making the world a better place

In advanced economies, today's consumers seek experiences that transcend the basics of food, shelter, and transportation. They seek new ways to meet essential needs that are less harmful to the environment, and greatly improved health treatments, and possible cures for the worst diseases. Examples include biodegradable plastic bottles, solar-powered homes, electric cars, and much more. A market-based economy is an extraordinarily complex system that evolves in response not only to changing consumer preferences but also to competition among firms, as well as to new laws and regulations.[25]

Consider an economy's productive capacity, as it exists today, as the sum of all tangible capital (buildings, machinery, land, and the like) and all intangible (including human) capital. Productive capacity primarily resides in the aggregate capital of all business firms, both private and public. It is noteworthy that in recent decades, more and more firms' market values greatly exceed the value of their tangible capital. This reflects the growing importance of intangible human capital that is mirrored in employees' creativity and their problem-solving skills, all of which fuel innovation. For example, Tesla Motors is the tip of the spear in disrupting the automotive industry. The firm produces advanced electric cars that, as yet, generate no profits. But Tesla's market value is huge due to investor expectations of future big consumer success that would bring big profits.

This kind of value creation should make hard-core environmentalists, as well as others, cheer both the free-market system that produces a firm like this as well as its employees whose skills result in the creation of substantial market value for its shareholders. Tesla's market value is the *result* of its perceived ability to deliver substantial benefits to consumers in the future. Needless to say, substantial gains in firms' market values are very good for society.

Now imagine a future stream of benefits to all consumers net of the cost to develop and deliver the benefits. Today's value of net benefits is similar conceptually to the total market value (equity, preferred stock, and debt owners) of all firms operating in today's economy. From this perspective, we can see that firms' market values are really quantitative gauges that correlate with the expected net benefits to society. On the other hand, these same market values are tied directly to the present value of firms' expected future net cash receipts.

In looking at firms from this perspective, it makes economic sense, as well as common sense, that Tesla Motors, led by Elon Musk, has a very large proportion of its market value tied to the value of its human capital while General Motors has a much lower proportion tied to its human capital. Similarly, Hewlett-Packard (HP) has struggled for many years to adapt to a fast-changing technological environment, while Illumina has dominated gene-sequencing technology. Compared to Illumina, the market value of HP reflects a far lower proportion of human capital that spurs innovation.

Clearly, increasing market values are highly desirable for investors but also to those who are focused solely on the benefits to society (economic progress) that make the world a better place. Lack of an insightful understanding of market valuation significantly impedes progress—important in the debate about the fundamental purpose of firms and the treatment of all stakeholders in a firm.

Stakeholders have a material interest in a firm and can affect its performance. A firm's stakeholders are many and include capital owners, employees, customers, suppliers, and local communities. Stakeholder theory is the viewpoint that a firm must be managed with concern for all stakeholders. That makes eminent sense. Properly managed, a firm should create value for all stakeholders. But how should management make decisions that involve multiple stakeholders with conflicting interests? Consistent with the above discussion about market valuation, Michael Jensen, a former professor at the Harvard Business School, provides an answer:

> The real issue is what corporate behavior will get the most out of society's limited resources—or equivalently, what behavior will result in the least social waste—not whether one group is or should be more privileged than another.
>
> ... Note that it is precisely because profit is the amount by which revenues exceed costs—by which the value of output exceeds the value of inputs—that profit maximization leads to an efficient social outcome.
>
> ... Value maximization (or value seeking) provides the following answer to the tradeoff question. Spend an additional dollar on any constituency provided the long-term value added to the firm from such expenditure is a dollar or more. Stakeholder theory, by contrast, contains no conceptual specification of how to make the tradeoffs among stakeholders.[26]

The problem is that *beginning* with maximizing shareholder value as the firm's purpose pushes aside the need to develop a purpose that *motivates* employees and other stakeholders to enthusiastically support the firm. The next section makes the case that achieving an appropriately defined purpose for the firm does reward shareholders over the long term.

What is the firm's purpose?

The three words "maximizing shareholder value" elicit a negative reaction from many people. They strongly believe the corporate goal of maximizing shareholder value has resulted in sky-high executive compensation tied to stock options that, in turn, promote an extreme focus on quarterly earnings to the detriment of a firm's long-term viability; large-scale employee layoffs even while top management paychecks are rising; health and environmental problems due to pressure on employees to do whatever it takes to "make the numbers"; accounting fraud; and the list goes on.

On the other side, proponents of maximizing shareholder value have an equally strong belief that the firm should, first and foremost, focus on profits. They often refer to Milton Friedman's famous 1970 essay "The Social Responsibility of Business Is to Increase its Profits," in which he says:

> … there is one and only one social responsibility of business—to use its resources and engage in activities designed to increase its profits so long as it stays within the rules of the game, which is to say, engages in open and free competition without deception or fraud.[27]

This is an emotionally charged debate that is probably best dealt with by first carefully defining the firm's purpose. Let's begin by noting that, to be effective, a firm's purpose needs to resonate with employees' higher-order beliefs of what is morally right and worth doing. A firm's purpose will be inspiring and motivating to employees if it is unambiguously perceived as worthy of the commitment of their working lives to achieve it.

The interrelated components of purpose

A firm's purpose should ideally tap into four core components that promote long-term business success and can be enthusiastically embraced by employees. The following components should be treated as a package deal that yields a holistic purpose for the firm:

1. **Have an inspiring vision**

   We will strive to fulfill the firm's vision while instilling high ethical standards throughout the firm.

2. **Survive and prosper**

   We will survive and prosper by delivering a level of efficiency and innovation that earns customer loyalty and rewards long-term shareholders.

3. **Create win–win relationships**

   We will strive for win–win relationships that provide value for those who partner with us in serving our customers.

4. **Care for future generations**

   We will take care of future generations by designing our products and services, and using our assets, consistent with environmental sustainability.

A visual summary of how achieving a firm's purpose translates into making the world a better place is displayed in Figure 3.1. Note that a firm's output, less the costs of all resources used, represents the net benefits to society identified in the bottom left side of the figure. Similar in concept, the bottom right side of the figure shows firms' market values driven by long-term net cash receipts, which are generated by providing value to customers.

From a quantitative perspective, the value of benefits received by society would seem to significantly exceed the value to the firms' capital owners (firms' market values). Although it is difficult to estimate precisely, Henry Ford's innovation and efficiencies in delivering an affordable automobile to consumers surely greatly exceeded the value delivered to his firm's capital owners. Consider also the new therapeutic drugs developed after the late 1980s to treat HIV/AIDS patients. The total profits generated by those new drugs for the pharmaceutical companies whose R&D produced them have been estimated at a mere 5 percent of the value of the total health benefits (longer lives) that patients gained. It is quite reasonable to assume that the scientists who worked late nights and weekends to develop these early drugs to treat HIV/AIDS were motivated, not by maximizing shareholder value, but rather by providing desperately needed health improvement to patients. Their successes resulted in value created for their firms' shareholders. Other research estimates that innovators, in general, capture only 2.2 percent of the total "surplus" from innovation. The surplus is the value to society less the cost of producing the innovation.[28]

Figure 3.1: Benefits to society and firms' market values

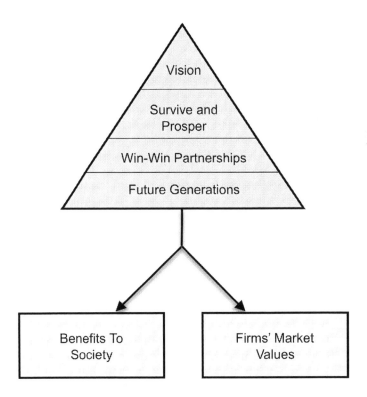

At the individual firm level, as long as it is inspirational and genuinely reflects how the firm is actually managed, a firm's vision or mission can be very broad. For example, consistent with its exceptionally diversified product portfolio, 3M's vision is, "3M technology advancing every company, 3M products enhancing every home, 3M innovation improving every life." Then there is Illumina management who have a unique vision, "to improve health by unlocking the power of the genome." These vision statements undeniably are aligned with making the world a better place.

A firm's very survival and prosperity depends on the management mind and managerial skill for orchestrating continuous efficiency gains and innovations. In life-cycle terminology, this is reflected in a favorable long-term fade rate of economic returns. To achieve such a favorable outcome, management should avoid empire-building mergers and acquisitions that are not wealth-creating for shareholders. Instead, the firm's reinvestment rates should be in response to wealth-creating opportunities that are suited to the firm's core capabilities. Instead of mega-mergers with dubious synergies, strategic acquisitions that expand core capabilities or add new capabilities can be a smart move.

However, firms first need to exist. Stakeholders don't start firms, entrepreneurs do. Keep in mind that efficiency and innovation needs to be management's ongoing top priority because nothing works if business economics fail. Adapting to a changing world requires hard-nosed managerial decisions that may well necessitate shutting down facilities and, at times, exiting current businesses. By contrast, highly successful firms invariably have developed win–win relationships with their partners/stakeholders in creating value. When a plant must be closed or a business unit divested, there are myriad ways to assist the impacted employees with a transition process that all employees will regard as the firm's doing the right thing.

One example of win–win relationships wherein management creates opportunities for stakeholders to create wealth is seen in Amazon's 2011 CEO letter to its shareholders:

> The most radical and transformative of inventions are often those that empower others to unleash their creativity— to pursue their dreams. That's a big part of what's going on with Amazon Web Services, Fulfillment by Amazon, and Kindle Direct Publishing.... we are creating powerful self-service platforms that allow thousands of people to boldly experiment and accomplish things that would otherwise be impossible or impractical. These innovative large-scale platforms are not zero-sum—they create win–win situations and create significant value for developers, entrepreneurs, customers, authors, and readers.[29]

Finally, concern for future generations is a powerful connection to employees' higher-order beliefs. Central to the concern about future generations is management's commitment to environmental sustainability. This also directly affects customers' perceptions of the firm that, over time, contributes to a firm's reputation. It is not about being on the razor's edge of just barely complying with Friedman's "rules of the game," e.g., environmental laws. It is about *designing* products, services, and manufacturing processes that truly minimize waste and harm to the environment. Such smart design can be profitable in financial terms as well as in enhancing the firm's reputation.

Beginning with a carefully defined purpose avoids the heated rhetoric and miscommunication surrounding the topic of maximizing shareholder value. Also, we would be positioning shareholder value over time as being the result of how well management delivers on the firm's four-part purpose.

Many years after Friedman penned his famous essay, there was a debate about capitalism in general and the role of business firms in particular. In addition to Friedman, John Mackey and T. J. Rodgers were participants. Mackey made the following points that are consistent with the spirit of the ideas in this chapter:

> Friedman is right to argue that profit making is intrinsically valuable for society, but I believe he is mistaken that all businesses have only this purpose. While Friedman believes that taking care of customers, employees, and business philanthropy are means to the end of increasing profits, I take the exact opposite view: Making high profits is the means to the end of fulfilling Whole Foods' core business mission. We want to improve the health and well-being of everyone on the planet through higher-quality foods and better nutrition, and we can't fulfill this mission unless we are highly profitable. High profits are necessary to fuel our growth across the United States and the world. Just as people cannot live without eating, so a business cannot live without profits. But most people don't live to eat, and neither must a business live just to make profits.
>
> … If we are truly interested in spreading capitalism throughout the world (I certainly am), we need to do a better job marketing it. I believe if economists and business people consistently communicated and acted on my message that "the enlightened corporation should try to create value for all of its constituencies," we would see most of the resistance to capitalism disappear.[30]

The core responsibilities of management

Given a firm's purpose, the next step is to gain clarity about management's responsibilities that are critical to achieving that purpose. The following three responsibilities, summarized in Figure 3.2, are the most essential ones for management to fulfill:

- To integrate an operationally useful valuation framework
- To use resources efficiently and to organize for continuous improvement
- To sustain a knowledge-building culture focused on innovation

These responsibilities focus on efficiency and innovation that determine a firm's degree of success in the competitive marketplace and, for that matter, whether or not the firm survives. Of course, many important managerial tasks are not addressed herein, such as environmental and health safeguards, customer satisfaction, employee engagement, stakeholder partnerships, and more. Performance of these tasks is increasingly being assisted via various types of balanced scorecards.

Figure 3.2: Three core responsibilities of management

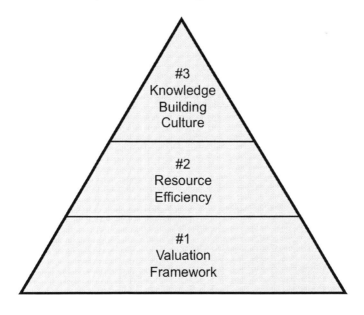

Management's first core responsibility involves the bedrock issue of how best to connect accounting data to valuation. *If management and boards are ever going to stop playing Wall Street's short-term quarterly earnings game, which is detrimental to long-term value creation, a prerequisite is to get comfortable with a conceptually sound and operationally useful valuation framework.* That will greatly help management assess the likely magnitude of long-term wealth creation or dissipation as it relates to major corporate decisions. In addition, it will assist them in understanding how a stock price truly represents *long-term* expectations of a firms' net cash receipt streams.

#1 To integrate an operationally useful valuation framework

The life-cycle valuation framework introduced in Chapter 2 will be explained in greater detail in Chapters 6 and 7. But before we get deep into details, let's focus here on the big picture. Management and boards need a *common language* to understand the past; develop wealth-creating strategies; analyze and make decisions about capital expenditures, acquisitions, divestitures; tie compensation to value creation; and communicate all this to investors. It is remarkable that, given the enormous importance of value creation, so many managements and boards lack an operationally useful tool to deal with value creation (or dissipation). Instead, earnings per share growth rates, market share, and other metrics are used as crude proxies for value creation.

The life-cycle valuation framework fulfills all these needs and is a logically sound application of discounted cash flow. Other valuation methodologies contain logically sound valuation calculations, too. However, the unique benefit provided by the life-cycle approach is the easy-to-comprehend visual display (Figure 2.1) of all the components used to articulate a forecasted net cash stream that is then discounted to a present value today. Techniques such as economic value added, or EVA® (a registered trademark of Stern Stewart & Co. and EVA Dimensions LLC), *compress* the component parts into a single number. But, it is more useful to be able to see the component parts.[31] EVA's gain in simplicity is offset by the loss of insights obtainable from analysis of historical charts of firms' life-cycle performance. Moreover, keep in mind that the mainstream finance procedure for assigning cost of capital produces enormously wide variations in answers based on different, but plausible, changes in assumptions. All this gets hidden behind a single EVA number. In addition, the explicit display of long-term data for both economic returns and reinvestment rates often reveals important strategic issues about levels and trends (fade rates), which also get lost by using the EVA methodology. These points are well known to portfolio managers who use the life-cycle framework to analyze historical company data. Managements and boards of directors would benefit from a similar experience of studying historical data.

The life-cycle valuation framework is especially useful in that it supports the following:

- Avoiding investments in businesses that are likely to earn economic returns below the cost of capital.
- Reinvesting in businesses that are likely to earn economic returns above the cost of capital.
- Developing strategies that can realistically produce favorable future fade rates.
- Experimenting with varied ways to handle intangibles and other tough accounting issues in order to improve the calculation of economic returns and to better understand business economics.
- Decoding investor expectations, which are embedded in current stock prices (see the Walmart example in Chapter 6).
- Explaining to investors why decisions were made that will penalize near-term quarterly earnings, but most likely will create shareholder value over the long term.

#2 To use resources efficiently and organize for continuous improvement

For a firm to survive and prosper over the long haul, it must achieve returns on capital that are at least equal to the investors' cost of capital. For resource efficiency, capital outlays should be consistent with this objective. The tie-in to shareholder value is quite direct. As illustrated in Chapter 6, the firm's value is composed of the present value of net cash receipts from *existing assets* plus the present value of *future investments*. The value of future investments is positive, zero, or negative depending on expected future ROIs' (return on investment) being above, equal to, or less than the cost of capital. Invest a dollar below the cost of capital and the market will value it at less than a dollar.

As to the efficiency of existing assets, there is a growing worldwide consensus that *lean thinking* (epitomized by the Japanese firm Toyota and the American firm Danaher) should be adopted in order to continually reduce waste and improve the efficiency of a firm's operations. In their book, *Lean Thinking: Banish Waste and Create Wealth in Your Corporation*, James Womack and Daniel Jones explain the five key lean principles as follows, "... precisely specify *value* by specific product, identify the *value stream* for each product, make value *flow* without interruptions, let the customer *pull* value from the producer, and pursue *perfection.*"[32]

Lean thinking is about a value stream perspective that is horizontal and cuts across the vertical silos that exist in the typical firm's organizational hierarchy. The goal is continual improvement in the processes that produce the accounting-based financial performance results. The idea is to improve constraints that degrade system performance and not get sidetracked into maximizing local accounting-based efficiencies of certain system components that fail to translate into performance gains for the overall system.

Accounting-based valuation of the firm and its major business units is essential, though accounting-based controls can be counterproductive at lower levels of the organization where the actual work gets done. So, instead, use process control variables at the lower levels. This point was emphasized by H. Thomas Johnson:

> No company that talks about improving performance can know what it is doing if its primary window on results is financial information and not system principles. No amount of financial manipulation will ever improve long-term results. Performance in the long run will improve only if managers ensure that the system from which the performance emerges adheres more and more closely to principles resembling those that guide the operations of a living system. The dilemma facing all companies that intend to become "lean" is that they can follow a truly systemic path to lean or they can continue to use management accounting "levers of control." They can't do both.[33]

It is quite tempting to "manage" accounting numbers instead of focusing on what really drives the results that eventually get measured by the accountants. This is a mistake and it produces bad outcomes, not only at the process level but also in capital outlay decision making. Recall at the end of Chapter 2 the Scott Cook quote in which he describes how new-product teams at Intuit in the early stage of developing new ideas postpone spreadsheet analysis and instead emphasize "where we can change lives most profoundly."

#3 To sustain a knowledge-building culture focused on innovation

A knowledge-building culture is essential for: continual process improvement in all areas of a firm's operations; development of wealth-creating long-term strategies; and orchestrating new investments that may utilize existing capabilities, or involve new capabilities, and possibly involve products and services sharply different from existing businesses. Toyota-style lean organizations have a culture that respects employee initiative and mentors employees to increase their problem-solving skills for process improvement. The hallmark of "lean" is systems thinking, experimentation, and learning. A systems mindset that is focused on identifying and fixing key constraints applies not only to the factory floor but also throughout the firm and even extends to customers. That is, find a way to eliminate an important constraint in a customer's business, and you have created a high-value new product.

Too often top management believes that merely installing "lean tools" and implementing occasional quality improvement programs is the path to a knowledge-building culture (learning organization). On the contrary, what is needed is a passionate commitment and ongoing participation by top management to knowledge building. The top-performing lean companies worldwide have a common characteristic—deep management involvement in lean as a way of life.[34]

Here is the hard part: We go through life experiencing what works and what doesn't. At any point in time our knowledge base, determined by our past experience, contains strongly held assumptions about cause and effect relationships. To get stuff done during the day we cannot be continually questioning our belief system (knowledge base). Top management gets to their senior level of responsibility because of their skill in making decisions based on their knowledge base. The difficulty is that the world keeps changing and some critical, strongly held assumptions become obsolete. If you study, as I have done, the CEO messages in annual reports spanning many years for firms as they fade to average, then to below-average, and then to bankruptcy/reorganization, you would observe CEOs who believed that what worked well for them in the past will continue to work well in the future. They were very late to recognize fundamental changes. Often too late.

Consequently, the challenge for management is to commit to a mindset that is constructively skeptical about critical business assumptions, and aware that the world is constantly changing in ways perceived dimly, if at all, at present, and therefore management makes a commitment to experimentation and feedback as a routine part of managing. Such a managerial mindset can yield a culture that "beats the fade"—a phrase used by professional money managers to describe companies that sustain economic returns well above the cost of capital and that do not follow the usual path of regression to the average. An excellent example of this type of culture and favorable fade is Intuit, which is analyzed in Chapter 8.

Figure 3.3 illustrates the connections among firms' purpose, management's core responsibilities, and a wealth-creation scorecard expressed via the life-cycle valuation framework.

Figure 3.3: Business firms and economic progress

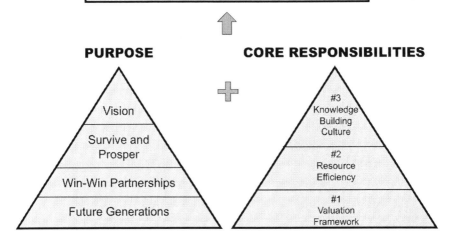

LIFE-CYCLE PERFORMANCE OBJECTIVE

- Economic returns above the cost of capital, and
- reinvestment rates supportive of maintaining a
- favorable long-term fade rate.

PURPOSE

- Vision
- Survive and Prosper
- Win-Win Partnerships
- Future Generations

CORE RESPONSIBILITIES

- #3 Knowledge Building Culture
- #2 Resource Efficiency
- #1 Valuation Framework

To sum up, there is a logical and useful connection between the firm's purpose and management's core responsibilities. But this rests on firms' operating in a free-market environment keyed to consumer choice as well as a level playing field for all competitors. But the growth of crony capitalism means that management is seizing more and more opportunities to use political means to increase their profitability and/or curtail new entrants into their industry. Of course, one way forward is for top managements and boards of directors to follow in the footsteps of T. J. Rodgers, CEO of Cypress Semiconductor, and refuse to lobby for special favors from Washington. Perhaps a more realistic way forward is for more and more top managements and boards to conclude that it is in everyone's best long-term interests to minimize the opportunities for crony capitalism for *all* firms in order to sustain a free-market society. How? Achieve structural reforms that take off the table opportunities to lobby for special favors (e.g., tax breaks). Start with an order-of-magnitude simpler tax code with a flat tax for corporations that has all investments expensed. This is economically sound and would eliminate a great many opportunities to lobby for special tax treatments.

Management should stop playing Wall Street's quarterly earnings game

To sustain a free-market society that nurtures long-term innovation by business firms, we need to turn back the rising tide of cronyism and its related corporate lobbying. For sure, this is a monumental task. A more doable objective in the near term is to nurture long-term innovation by having management and boards stop playing Wall Street's quarterly earnings game. In this game, management puts its employees under intense pressure to at least meet, or preferably exceed, Wall Street's expectations for quarterly earnings. If you think that would motivate all sorts of bad behavior, including creative accounting manipulations, you would be right.[35]

Why does this situation exist? It exists because of the widespread lack of an operationally useful valuation framework that is integrated through-out the firm, most especially at the top management and board levels. It reflects a lack of integrity that casts a blind eye to accounting manipula-tions as part of doing whatever it takes to hit accounting targets. A useful valuation framework is needed to facilitate logical analysis and empirical evidence to persuade management to break the chokehold of quarterly earnings expectations.

To be sure, measuring progress toward important goals is essential and quarterly reports do provide relevant information to investors. But avoiding long-term, wealth-creating investments that would penalize near-term quarterly earnings is an all too common result of the quarterly earnings cycle. You would think that Chief Financial Officers (CFOs), whose job it is to be skilled in understanding wealth creation issues, would be leading the charge to encourage top management to make wealth-cre-ating, long-term investments even if this entails a reduction in near-term quarterly results; and to explain all this to investors. You would be wrong.

There are many discounted cash flow valuation models in use that plainly reveal that stock prices actually represent very long-term forecasts of future net cash receipts. Further, academic studies reaffirm this con-clusion, which is well documented in corporate finance textbooks. CFOs know this. Nevertheless, Professors John Graham and Campbell Har-vey at Duke University and Professor Shiva Rajgopal at the University of Washington report genuinely disturbing findings about CFOs in their aptly entitled article "Value Destruction and Financial Reporting Deci-sions." Based on a survey of 401 senior financial executives they report:

> Results … indicate that 80 percent of survey participants
> would decrease discretionary spending (e.g., R&D, advertis-
> ing, maintenance) to meet an earnings target, even though
> many CFOs acknowledge that suboptimal maintenance
> and other spending can be value destroying. More than half

of the CFOs (55.3 percent) said they would delay starting a new project to meet an earnings target, even if such a delay entailed a sacrifice in value. This evidence is interesting because CFOs appear to be willing to burn "real" cash flows for the sake of reporting desired accounting numbers.[36]

The question becomes just what are CFOs controlling for with this behavior? CFOs answered that their behavior was consistent with their model of stock price change. Their *operational valuation model* is: stock price changes move in lockstep with quarterly earnings' being above or below expectations. Moreover, they perceived their behavior as necessary to advance their careers. In other words, their marketability in the job market is perceived as being determined by their "performance" in delivering quarterly results that hit the right note, according to the tune that Wall Street wants to hear.

A corporate culture of doing whatever it takes to meet Wall Street's short-term expectations is diametrically opposed to the real purpose of the firm (previously discussed), which is all about creating long-term value. And with such a culture, management typically ignores its responsibility to integrate an operationally useful valuation framework—useful for dealing with the level of market valuations and not merely short-term changes.

There is a better way. CFOs and the CEOs they report to should make decisions as if they themselves are both significant owners of a privately held company. With that mindset, they would both want to build long-term value and would frown upon the short-term behavior noted above. Rather than striving for membership in Wall Street's do-whatever-it-takes quarterly earnings club, they would want membership in the beat-the-fade club. In summary, society benefits (Figure 3.3) when management delivers outstanding performance over many years in delivering economic returns and reinvestment rates that exceed earlier investor expectations. The result is a rising relative wealth index—seen in the bottom panel in the life-cycle company charts in this book. Let's take a look at how Amazon became a member of the beat-the-fade club.

Membership in the beat-the-fade club: Amazon

Amazon's vision is to be Earth's most customer-centric company where people can find and discover anything they might want to buy online. Amazon began as an online book store. Today, it leads the Internet-based retailing industry with a wide diversity of product offerings, including its own brand of consumer electronic products. Amazon's information technology skills were leveraged via Amazon Web Services, which has earned a large share of the cloud infrastructure services industry. Today, Amazon has a higher equity market valuation than Walmart.

Amazon's founder and CEO, Jeff Bezos, is an off-the-chart builder of long-term value. It is difficult to name a large company that currently would be rated higher than Amazon in terms of an obsession with customer satisfaction. Amazon is an innovation machine for delivering value to customers—often in novel ways that break with industry convention such as Bezos' decision to allow negative product reviews on Amazon's website in order to build long-term customer trust. Bezos summarizes his view about Amazon's uniqueness as follows:

> If you want to get to the truth about what makes us dif-
> ferent, it's this: We are genuinely customer-centric, we
> are genuinely long-term oriented and we genuinely like
> to invent. Most companies are not those things. They are
> focused on the competitor, rather than the customer. They
> want to work on things that will pay dividends in two or
> three years, and if they don't work in two or three years
> they will move on to something else. And they prefer to be
> close-followers rather than inventors, because it's safer. So
> if you want to capture the truth about Amazon, that is why

we are different. Very few companies have all of those three elements.[37]

Amazon's 1997 annual report letter to shareholders contained the following comments by Bezos, which should be posted on the office walls of the previously discussed CFOs who are intent on doing whatever it takes to hit Wall Street's short-term targets:

> We first measure ourselves in terms of the metrics most indicative of our market leadership: customer and revenue growth, the degree to which our customers continue to purchase from us on a repeat basis, and the strength of our brand …
>
> We will continue to make investment decisions in light of long-term market leadership considerations rather than short-term profitability considerations or short-term Wall Street reactions …
>
> We will make bold rather than timid investment decisions where we see a sufficient probability of gaining market leadership advantages …
>
> When forced to choose between optimizing the appearance of our GAAP accounting and maximizing the present value of future cash flows, we'll take the cash flows …
>
> We believe that a fundamental measure of our success will be the shareholder value we create over the long term.[38]

In the life-cycle chart in Figure 3.4, you can see that Amazon's shareholder returns have greatly exceeded the S&P 500 Index (rising relative wealth line in the lower panel) after an early downdraft when the company was getting started. Amazon has substantially beat the fade.

Figure 3.4: Amazon

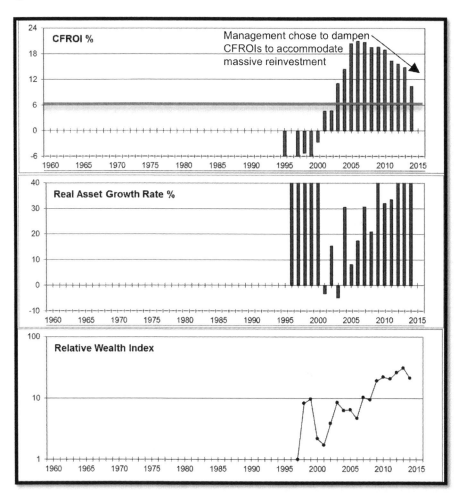

Source: Credit Suisse HOLT global database

Normally a firm beats the fade when it delivers *rising* economic returns that exceed early investor expectations. Amazon is different. The key insight into Amazon's outperformance in the stock market comes from the asset growth rates displayed in the middle panel of the figure. As firms grow larger, competitors typically invest in ways that reduce the opportunities for a firm such as Amazon to reinvest in wealth-creating projects. Hence, a firm's reinvestment rate in its asset base regresses (fades) toward a slower economy-type growth rate. But Amazon's reinvestment rate has been sustained at an exceptionally high level that exceeded early investor expectations and has been the primary cause of Amazon's stock beating the fade. Importantly, the decline in CFROIs has been due to massive reinvestment in new ventures that depressed the solid profitability of Amazon's core businesses. Note that the combination of sustained high reinvestment rates with high economic returns is the path to unusually large wealth creation. This is similar to the first two decades of Walmart (analyzed in Chapter 6). Although Amazon has had its share of failures, some of the new projects develop into very successful businesses that, in turn, make Amazon's website platform even more useful to its customers. With ever-increasing scale, a competitive moat gets strengthened and further extends a firm's ability to beat the fade in the future.

Getting back to the dual managerial challenge of continuous productivity improvement for existing businesses and innovations to meet tomorrow's customer needs, Bezos notes that about 70 percent of Amazon's innovation expenditures are focused on process improvements to their existing businesses. The remainder is focused on funding potential large-scale new businesses. For example, the Kindle e-book reader has been a revolutionary development in delivering value to those who read books while expanding the marketplace for books by reducing their cost. Returning to Amazon's obsession with customer needs, Bezos explains the process involved with radical innovations such as the Kindle:

> Companies get skills-focused, instead of customer-needs focused. When [companies] think about extending their business into some new area, the first question is "why should we do that—we don't have any skills in that area."

That approach puts a finite lifetime on a company, because the world changes, and what used to be cutting-edge skills have turned into something your customers may not need anymore. A much more stable strategy is to start with "what do my customers need?" Then do an inventory of the gaps in your skills. Kindle is a great example. If we set our strategy by what our skills happen to be rather than by what our customers need, we never would have done it. We had to go out and hire people who know how to build hardware devices and create a whole new competency for the company.[39]

The comments above about innovation say a great deal about the kind of managerial mindset needed to beat the fade for an extended period.

PART II:
A KNOWLEDGE-BUILDING CULTURE IS CRITICAL TO A FIRM'S LONG-TERM SURVIVAL AND SUCCESS

CHAPTER 4

The Pivotal Role of Worldviews in Building Knowledge

By detaching our self-image and self-worth from our beliefs, we should be more willing to stress test those beliefs instead of habitually defending them. This means that being who we are won't be tied up in maintaining a particular view, answer, opinion, or conclusion. Rather, we can define our "being" by how we think and converse. Defining everything we know as conditional—subject to change based on new evidence—can help decouple our egos from our beliefs. To be good critical thinkers requires intellectual humility and a healthy respect for the magnitude of what we don't know.
—Edward D. Hess[40]

We live in language in the same way that fish live in water: it is transparent to us. It's not that we don't know that we speak and listen, but rather we are unaware that language is shaping the world as we see it. When we see the sky after an astronomer shares with us distinctions about celestial bodies, we are able to see what we were unable to see before that conversation. We see galaxies, planets, and satellites where before there were only a bunch of "stars."

—Julio Olalla[41]

It is customary in business articles and books to describe *best practices* for a wide variety of business operations. However, what is typically neglected to be mentioned is the most fundamental and important of the best practices, and that is the quick and efficient building of useful knowledge, i.e., get smarter. That is the topic of this chapter.

Humility and a healthy respect for what we don't know is a cornerstone for building knowledge and improving our problem-solving skills. Economic progress is about solving important problems and scaling up the solutions so many people can benefit. Every employee in a firm has some capability to solve problems, which improves by building up their knowledge base. Of course, this is contingent on how different contexts can change the consequences of the actions they take. So, it is useful to first gain clarity about the knowledge-building process and then to focus on ways to improve that process. In this chapter, the knowledge-building process is analyzed in the form of a knowledge-building loop. An important component of the loop is one's worldview. A plausible case is presented that adopting the four core beliefs presented in this chapter will upgrade one's worldview, thereby leading to substantial gains in knowledge and working smarter.

The four core beliefs are used at the end of this chapter to understand why Michelin's run-flat tire innovation was a commercial failure and why an improved management worldview could have avoided this huge financial loss.

The world you see

Our senses continually receive an avalanche of signals from the external environment. To avoid sensory overload, our brains function much of the time in autopilot mode. Evolution favors efficiency, so our brains have evolved to enable subconscious, fast processing of information that does not require conscious (energy-using) processing. Consistent with its energy-thrifty ways, our brains store and use past experiences to further facilitate making predictions about future events. The neuropsychologist Richard Gregory put it this way:

> For perception, there is always guessing and going beyond available evidence. On this view, the closest we ever come to the object world is by somewhat uncertain hypotheses, selected from present evidence and enriched by knowledge from the past. Some of this knowledge is inherited— learned by the statistical processes of natural selection and stored by the genetic code. The rest is brain-learning from individual experience, especially important for humans.[42]

The neuroscientist Chris Frith summarizes it as follows:

> By hiding from us all the unconscious inferences it makes, our brain creates the illusion that we have direct contact with objects in the physical world.... What I perceive are not the crude and ambiguous cues that impinge from the outside world onto my eyes and my ears and my fingers. I perceive something much richer—a picture that combines all these crude signals with a wealth of past experience. My perception is a prediction of what ought to be out there in the world. And this prediction is constantly tested by action.[43]

Through the integration of past experiences, we hypothesize and confirm (or refute) how things work by treating the majority of things as independent realities. We are accustomed to using simple linear cause and effect thinking—if X, then Y—because it works so well in our everyday lives. But that reliability has primarily to do with nonliving things, which are devoid of purpose. When one billiard ball hits another, the effect is easy to predict.

The key point here may sound philosophical, but it is of huge practical importance. Reality exists within the context of purposeful human behavior. Such a viewpoint does not require the denial of a real world. Rather, it explicitly recognizes our *participation* in shaping the world we see as real.[44]

As for the practical task of solving a problem, it follows that how a problem is perceived, the initial selection of variables likely to be important, the first hunch at how these variables might be related, and the criteria used for evaluating the evolving hypotheses do not arise in an unbiased manner. Our past experiences have produced a web of strongly held assumptions that are so ingrained in us that we typically are not even conscious of their influence on us. The result is that we consider ourselves to be independent of problem situations—objective problem solvers. Moreover, the language we use tends to make us comfortable in our belief about our objectivity. Language plays a major role in how we experience the world.

The uniqueness of something meriting a name implies that the thing has an independent existence—independent of both context and purposeful behavior. Consequently, paying attention to the assumptions behind the words can be highly productive for almost any type of research question, ranging from new product ideas to incremental process improvements. As our knowledge increases, typically our language becomes more precise. Note how the medical profession is transitioning away from terms such as "lung cancer" and "breast cancer" in order to more precisely identify the type of tumor involved. To sum up, developing genuine insights and resolving problems is helped by close scrutiny of how we participate in perceiving the world and, especially, how we use language.

Knowledge-building loop

On one hand, language can constrain our vision and interfere with knowledge building. On the other hand, language can be the pathway to discovering flawed assumptions and dealing with root causes of problems. Figure 4.1 displays the knowledge-building process as interrelated components—every component influenced by language. The knowledge-building loop applies to any kind of learning experience, from a marketing person who wants to improve his or her hit rate in converting sales leads to confirmed orders to a scientist grappling with understanding, and hopefully curing, a deadly disease.

Figure 4.1: Knowledge-building loop

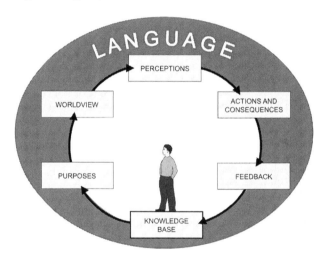

Source: Bartley J. Madden, "Management's Worldview: Four Critical Points about Reality, Language, and Knowledge Building to Improve Organization Performance," Journal of Organizational Computing and Electronic Commerce *22 (4): 334–46.*

The knowledge-building loop provides a useful roadmap to follow Edward Jenner's path to develop the smallpox vaccine. In the 18th century, people lived in fear of a deadly disease called smallpox. Edward

Jenner, a medical doctor in England, spent twenty years developing his knowledge base about smallpox, a process that led to preventive vaccination and the eventual eradication of this disease.

Referring to Figure 4.1, the medical establishment and Jenner shared a common *purpose*, i.e., how best to help people avoid smallpox, which was often fatal, and those who did survive frequently suffered terrible scarring or blindness. Jenner's *worldview* (i.e., his ideas and beliefs for interpreting and interacting with the world) differed markedly from those of many of his medical colleagues. Jenner had a passion for observing and studying nature. His mentor was John Hunter, a noted scientist, who instilled in him the importance of generating hypotheses and experimenting.[45]

Consider the different *perceptions* made by Jenner versus the medical establishment on hearing milkmaids claim they did not get smallpox because they were protected by prior exposure to cowpox. Due to their milking cows, milkmaids would occasionally get cowpox, which was a mild disease that produced pus-filled blisters on their hands for a few weeks. Jenner was immediately interested in further investigation, while other doctors dismissed the idea. The other doctors pointed out that some milkmaids who were exposed to cowpox subsequently avoided smallpox, but others still got it. Moreover, the other doctors' worldview was so constrained that they simply could not allow for the possibility that a cow disease could protect against a human disease.

But Jenner's perception of the milkmaid situation immediately led him to focus on observing *actions and consequences*—specifically, how the action of exposure to cowpox sometimes had the consequence of giving immunity from smallpox. Jenner was skeptical about the perception of "exposure" versus the reality of "exposure." With a honed, scientific way of thinking, he was keenly aware that the use of language and our perception of reality are intertwined. To Jenner, "exposure" was not a fact, but a fruitful area for investigation. Through experimentation, he discovered that there were many cowpox-like diseases, but only one could protect against smallpox. Then he discovered that it was the large, bluish blisters that occurred midway through the cowpox cycle that contained pus potent enough to protect against smallpox. Jenner's observations and experiments provided *feedback* to him that, over time, continually improved his *knowledge base.*

Clearly, Jenner's worldview facilitated his investigation of new relationships that did not fit within existing medical knowledge—much more so than the worldviews of many of his medical colleagues. It is noteworthy that he submitted a paper reporting his findings to England's Royal Society and received this reply, "... would more likely keep his colleagues' esteem in this respectable society by withdrawing his manuscript and forgetting about it as quickly as possible."[46] That faulty perception of his work was soon forgotten in the wake of demonstrated health benefits from following Jenner's recommendations. Vaccine technology improved over time and in 1967 the World Health Organization began a campaign to totally eradicate smallpox. In 1977, the last person to become infected with smallpox was reported in Somalia, Africa.

As it is the lens through which you interpret and interact with the world, your worldview holds enormous leverage for either restraining or expediting knowledge building. Worldviews are important because they affect how we see (perceive) the world. A deficient worldview (Figure 4.1), rooted in strongly held but obsolete assumptions, interferes with fast and effective learning experiences (loops) involving perceptions, actions, and consequences, plus feedback. Yet a sharpened worldview facilitates knowledge-building experiences that can reveal important insights critical for problem solving and for innovation in general. Four core beliefs have the potential to significantly upgrade your worldview. The following descriptions are a shortened version of a more comprehensive discussion to be found in my book *Reconstructing Your Worldview: The Four Core Beliefs You Need To Solve Complex Business Problems.*

Core Belief 1: Past experiences shape assumptions

Core Belief 1: Our perceptions are rooted in assumptions that are based on what has proved useful in the past and are typically based on an application of linear cause-and-effect analysis (if X, then Y). However, an automatic reliance on our assumptions can inadvertently lead to bad decisions, especially so whenever a significant change in context occurs.

For a revealing example of the strong pull of past experience, let's go back in time to the early 1970s when Kmart was the dominant retailer in the United States. From 1960 to 1972, Kmart's stock price outperformed the S&P 500 36-fold as its management successfully introduced the discount department store concept. By the early 1970s, Kmart management believed they had a proven business model and viewed the future as a continuation of past success. They did not pay much attention to Sam Walton—an entrepreneur in Arkansas with a few retail stores and a knack for fast learning and seeing through status-quo assumptions.

Sam Walton's fledging retail business eventually grew into Walmart and along the way sent Kmart into bankruptcy. Of particular importance was an early insight Walton had that led to a business strategy opposite to Kmart's strategy. Sam Walton decided to locate big stores in *small towns* such that Walmart's profitability would be tied to providing value to a neglected segment of the retail industry. In addition, he figured that population growth would eventually reach his stores. Kmart saw its profitability tied to operating big stores in *big towns,* which would presumably lead to high operating leverage. The root cause of this divergence resides in two different assumptions. Kmart management assumed that a store was an independent entity with store managers having responsibility for all operating decisions. That assumption came from their business success in the past. Sam Walton had a different view. He assumed that a *store is a node in an interconnected business system.* Everything changes with this assumption.[47]

With superior logistics tied to the placement of both its warehouses and its stores plus centralized ordering and control of inventory, Walmart was able to improve the efficiency of its operations at a far faster pace than Kmart and other competitors. Walmart's culture emphasized fast and inexpensive testing (knowledge building) followed by rapid implementation. Fast learning and attention to detail was in Walmart's DNA. For example, computer programmers were required to first perform the tasks for which they were going to write code in order to improve a business process. Details matter.

Substantial wealth can be created when management sees that an industry-wide assumption is faulty and can be exploited. Sam Walton identified significant inefficiencies with the status quo view of a stand-alone store controlled by a store manager. Instead, he focused on *growing and controlling a system of stores.* He noted:

> But while the big guys were leapfrogging from large city to large city, they became so spread out and so involved in real estate and zoning laws and city politics that they left huge pockets of business out there for us. Our growth strategy was born out of necessity, but at least we recognized it as a strategy pretty early on. We figured we had to build our stores so that our distribution centers, or warehouses, could take care of them, but also so those stores could be controlled. We wanted them within reach of our district managers ... Each store had to be within a day's drive of a distribution center.[48]

Core Belief 2: Language is perception's silent partner

Core Belief 2: Our perceptions, our thinking, and our use of language are intertwined to such a degree that unraveling the assumptions behind the words can be a useful step in building knowledge. This also facilitates a creative use of language to generate new opportunities for a future unshackled from obsolete assumptions.

We participate, through assumptions derived from past experience, in creating our reality, i.e., what we perceive. Why do we invariably overlook the role of assumptions? The reason has to do with language. Words promote an independent existence to what is named. Words facilitate rapid cause and effect analyses, providing a comfortable sense of certainty. Hence, language lulls us into believing that facts speak for themselves and that our initial perceptions of situations are reliable. To humankind's benefit, Edward Jenner questioned what was involved when people used the word "exposure," and this led him to a cure for smallpox. Sam Walton was open to new possibilities about the meaning of the word "store." Meanwhile, his type of curiosity and imagination was clearly not present in the top ranks of Kmart management.

Language is a pathway to the discovery of faulty assumptions and to ways of reformulating problems that yield insightful solutions. Language is much more than the means to communicate with words and symbols, either written or spoken. We communicate in subtle ways, including body language. Language is an integral part of the knowledge-building process depicted in the Knowledge-Building Loop seen in Figure 4.1. Recall the quote at the beginning of this chapter, "... When we see the sky after an astronomer shares with us *distinctions* about celestial bodies, we are able to see what we were unable to see before that conversation."

The knowledge-building process that yielded those distinctions involved perceiving and overthrowing old assumptions that were no longer fruitful. The scientists had conversations among themselves that produced an improved knowledge base. In the case of astronomy, communicating one's interpretations of visual data is critical. As conversations become more productive, new distinctions can emerge and be given mathematical symbols and words. Language participates in the process that results in a researcher's discovering new distinctions.[49]

Often we tend to associate high intelligence with verbal language skill. However, this can be misleading because a person's intellectual output is a function of their skill in navigating the entire knowledge-building loop. Moreover, those with exceptional visual/spatial skill and concomitant sharpened perceptual skill might be lacking verbal skill. Michael Faraday was self-educated and gained the reputation as the greatest experimental scientist of the 19th century. He unlocked the mystery of electromagnetism but did not possess the mathematical skill needed to broadly communicate his revolutionary insights to the scientific community. James Clerk Maxwell had visual/spatial expertise similar to Faraday's. He immediately fully appreciated Faraday's new paradigm. Maxwell translated Faraday's insights into mathematical language, i.e., the famous Maxwell equations; and he always pointed out that Faraday was the original source. Maxwell had severe speech problems and was a stutterer throughout his life. Today, based on his overall scientific accomplishments, Maxwell is ranked up there with Newton and Einstein.

In business as well as science, innovative thinking is about conceptualizing the big picture and uncovering connections that heretofore have not been visible. That process improves as we sharpen our worldview with an awareness that we participate in shaping our reality and that language can be either an impediment or a useful tool to improve our knowledge base. While breakthrough innovations are synonymous with creativity, managerial creativity is especially needed for the all-too-familiar problem of orchestrating change in situations where management and employees never seem to get on the same page. Consequently, big gains in performance are on the horizon but remain elusive.

Two ideas are relevant to handling situations that involve deep-seated behavioral problems. First, what we are not aware of (e.g., a new and better future) affects what we see and feel, which, in turn, affects our level of commitment and enthusiasm for work. Second, language is a pathway to helping employees rid themselves of strongly held beliefs that the future will necessarily be a continuation of an undesirable past. Management's challenge is to use these ideas in such a way that employees perceive a future purged of obsolete assumptions that would have constricted their future to be a continuation of an undesirable past. This is illustrated in Figure 4.2.

Figure 4.2: A future unshackled from the past

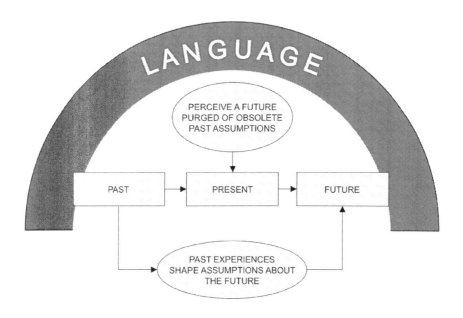

In their book, *The Three Laws of Performance: Rewriting the Future of Your Organization and Your Life,* Steve Zaffron, CEO of the Vanto Group, and Dave Logan, senior partner of CultureSync, summarize their decades of experience helping management change employees' perceptions about the future and thereby secure substantial gains in organizational performance. Here is a highly condensed version of their three laws of performance:

1. *How people perform correlates to how situations occur to them.* Strongly held assumptions, based on past experience, lay out a future that *is* your reality. Performance then conforms to this reality.

2. *How a situation occurs arises in language.* Zaffron and Logan emphasize that:
   Language is the means through which your future is already written. It is also the means through which it can be rewritten.... Untying the knots of language begins with seeing that whenever you say something, other communication is carried along with it.... The unsaid is the most important part of language when it comes to elevating performance.

3. *Future-based language transforms how situations occur to people.* Zaffron and Logan explain the steps needed as follows:
   ... seeing that what binds and constrains us isn't the facts, it's language ... issues that lurk in the unsaid occur as facts. When we become aware of these issues and are able to address and articulate them, what had occurred to us as facts shifts to being interpretations.
   ... articulating the default future and asking, "Do we really want this as our future?"
   ... completing issues from the past.

The insights briefly described above are, in my opinion, unusually powerful because they help upgrade one's worldview with exceedingly broad applicability to problem situations, especially business problems.[50]

This is unlike the typical management book that describes an author's observations about certain characteristics of management that, if duplicated, will presumably lead to high performance in the future. The problems with this line of thinking are covered in Chapter 8.

Core Belief 3: Improve performance by identifying and fixing a system's key constraints

> **Core Belief 3: Systems thinking is invaluable as a means to complement linear cause-and-effect analysis applied to isolated components of a system, to address the tendency toward an excessive focus on local efficiencies that can easily degrade overall system performance, and to powerfully identify and focus on fixing the key constraints to achieving the system goal.**

We go through life seeking certainty so we can gain a measure of control over our lives. We rely on logical (linear) cause-and-effect analysis. So, when managers achieve a position of responsibility they are already well conditioned to exercise control by breaking apart any complexity encountered into its component parts and then measuring the performance of those individual components to the overall system. Keep in mind that there is a commonsense basis for a hierarchical organization that, for example, separates a sales department from manufacturing or R&D. However, relying solely on linear thinking can easily result in a worldview that focuses in the extreme on individual components isolated from the overall system.

In business, control has become synonymous with accounting data. In a command-and-control hierarchical organization, management uses accounting-based goals and budgets to control performance. Deviations from accounting targets are seen as problems that need to be fixed, and the sooner the better. That accounting costs should be reduced in order to improve performance is a strongly entrenched belief widely held by management.

However, reductions in accounting costs *automatically* translate to improved overall system performance *only if* we assume that components of the system are independent of one another. What is needed is a worldview that embraces systems thinking and questions actions that are geared to improve local efficiencies without regard for the impact on the overall system. What follows is an especially critical point. On one hand, management wants to nurture a culture of continuous improvement in which employees are routinely engaged in learning how to improve productivity using process variables to measure that progress. On the other hand, management typically uses accounting data to make top-down capital expenditure decisions that target productivity improvements. Later, they are often disappointed with the results. Why? The illusory productivity improvement can be explained by way of a simple example where machine A feeds into machine B. With B being the bottleneck, the installation of a faster and more efficient machine at A will make a bad situation at B even worse. While accounting-based performance (cost per unit produced) at A improved, overall system performance declined. Management should have first given their attention to identifying the *key constraint* in the overall system and directed resources to eliminating that constraint. Then repeat the process. For example, if a major manufacturing constraint has been resolved, output can then surge and the new key constraint can then have moved to marketing. Contrast this to a worldview focused in the extreme on reducing accounting costs. From that perspective, there are opportunities to reduce accounting costs *everywhere and at all times*. Far better for management to gain genuine leverage by directing resources to specific bottlenecks (key constraints) that exist at specific points in time.[51]

Everything changes for management when they embrace systems

thinking. Let's begin with how management *sees* their firm. Managers who have embraced systems thinking and practice the lean principles epitomized by the Toyota Production System are on a mission to reduce waste (non-value-added activities), which includes both materials and time. Systems thinkers do not view work processes with a *vertical* frame of reference tied to accounting data for various silos in the firm's organization.[52] Rather, they use a *horizontal* perspective that focuses on *value streams* for products, i.e., all the activities involved with the design, production, delivery, servicing, and recycling of a product. And that includes the activities of their firm's suppliers, as well.

At Toyota plants, employees are mentored to continually improve operating efficiency within a culture that actually seeks to identify problems and discover root causes in order to permanently eliminate undesirable effects. The Toyota culture, where supervisors are more like coaches, enables employees to achieve significant satisfaction from developing problem-solving skills attuned to dealing with uncertainty. This is in sharp contrast to a culture of doing whatever it takes to make the accounting targets, with employees relying on supervisors to devise work-arounds and assorted fire-fighting routines. Within that type of culture, employees are limited in the growth of their problem-solving skills and limited in job satisfaction.

The systems way of thinking neatly fits with the knowledge-building loop (Figure 4.1) and has wide applicability beyond manufacturing plants. In particular, the concept of focusing on key constraints has wide applicability. A firm's customers have key constraints in their own work processes and are highly receptive to innovative solutions. As consumers, who among us has not experienced significant waste in terms of money and time in trying to get a product/service to do what is expected? Again, these are opportunities for developing innovative solutions.

Especially valuable is a systems perspective that uncovers a faulty assumption—an assumption so ingrained that it is almost never questioned. When a faulty assumption is widely held within an industry and not easily abandoned, the stage is set for an innovator to earn economic returns well above the cost of capital. Such was the case for an innovation that fundamentally reorganized how work gets done in distribution warehouses.

The entrepreneurs who started Kiva Systems applied systems thinking to the organization of large distribution warehouses. The key constraint to improving productivity at warehouses was the time needed for employees to locate and retrieve the items to be shipped. Note that the hidden assumption behind the words *locate and retrieve* is that employees move to the items. The Kiva insight was that robotic shelves could be designed to move the items to the employees—the exact opposite of industry practice. Additionally, software could keep track of orders to be filled and optimally schedule how the robotic shelves reach the employees. Amazon acquired Kiva Systems in 2012. Before Kiva robotic shelves were in operation, Amazon employees processed about 100 items per hour. After the robotic shelves were operational, employees processed about 300 items per hour.

Core belief 3 is particularly useful to management in order to fulfill its responsibilities to use resources efficiently and to sustain a knowledge-building culture.

Core Belief 4: Behavior is control of perception

Core Belief 4: Human behavior is purposeful, so it can be productively analyzed as a living control system that acts to maintain the perceptions of important variables as close as possible to preferred levels. In short, behavior is control of perception. A control perspective reveals the underlying weakness in viewing the world primarily as stimulus–response experiences.

A major part of managing a firm involves motivating employees, deeply understanding customer needs, building win–win relationships, and other people-oriented tasks. As such, what theory is most useful for dealing with human behavior? A very appealing theory relies on our life experiences with linear cause and effect. Previously, it was noted that a cause and effect framework was ideally suited to nonliving things. Nevertheless, it has proven so useful to us in the past that we rarely question it as the method of choice. Consequently, we tend to adopt a stimulus (cause)–response (effect) theory for dealing with human behavior. That is, we see behavior as basically a response to an external stimulus. In many instances this approach can and does works. Who has not offered a piece of candy (stimulus) to a child in exchange for the child's doing something (response) we want them to do?

But a theory is a source of big problems when it proves useful in certain contexts but not in others—especially problematic when we do not know beforehand which contexts are suitable for applying this particular theory. That is the underlying issue with the stimulus–response approach to human behavior. There is an answer to this dilemma. It is called Perceptual Control Theory (PCT), which was developed by William T. Powers. Over the past few decades, PCT has been quietly gaining support as a new paradigm for the social sciences. But its widespread adoption has been held back due to the entrenched methodology of academic research focused on stimulus–response empirical studies using variables that typically are straightforward to measure. PCT-based empirical research is challenging because the variables people are controlling for are typically not easily observable.

PCT's key idea is that we humans are wired as hierarchical control systems. Such systems have higher, slower-acting levels that guide lower, faster-acting levels. Life is about a continual process of controlling—or trying to control—what we experience. That is, we compare our actual experience to our preferred experience and, as needed, we take action to get our experience to match what we want. The difference between what we want and our actual experience is labeled error in PCT terminology. Consequently, control is a process of reducing error.[53]

Let's look at a highly simplified, stylized example of the key components of PCT. It is a cold winter's day and you open a window (stimulus) in your living room. Soon, warm air (response) enters the room through vents in the floor. A person unaware of the role thermostats play would be inclined to think opening the window *caused* the furnace to deliver heat. From a linear cause and effect perspective, this makes sense and its reliability is demonstrated by repeating this procedure at various times of day. But, reliability disappears when a new context is introduced in which the thermostat's desired room temperature is set very low (reference setting). In this context, the action of opening a window would not promptly be followed by a rush of hot air out of the vents.

It is important to note that our actions have purpose—that our perception of a *controlled variable* should move closer to the *reference setting* for that variable. As previously noted, the temperature we desire and set is the reference setting in the thermostat example. Powers' Perceptual Control Theory views living organisms (not just humans) as equipped with a *hierarchical organization* of control systems that operate using *negative feedback control*. In other words, a difference between our desired perception (reference setting) and actual perception motivates action on our part to *reduce the error*. Feedback is negative in the sense that it reduces error. The critical insight is that behavior is best understood, not as responses to external stimuli, but as control of perception.

There is much more to PCT's view of your brain's functioning as a hierarchy of control systems than can be adequately covered in this chapter. At the highest level of the hierarchy is your worldview that involves your strongest-held beliefs when it comes to understanding your life experiences. Your worldview is the lens for interpreting and interacting with the world. A hierarchical organization of control is extraordinarily efficient because higher-order goals set reference conditions for lower-level systems, enabling lower-level control to operate very quickly to reduce error. Think of all the instantaneous actions you take while driving a car without having to think about what to do.[54]

Perceptual control theory is helpful for managing people. To understand behavior we need to view a person from the inside out and concern ourselves with their control variables (goals), especially variables deemed very important (higher order) in an individual's hierarchical control system. Importantly, when we know a person's goals, we usually can predict the consequences of their actions although we may not be able to predict the actions taken. Successful change for an individual, group, or organization has to do with achieving the desired consequences from actions.

Management should strive to align employees' goals with management's goals. Employees need to feel their work is making a meaningful contribution toward adding value to a business process. And that process is an essential part of achieving the firm's mission. The mission should ideally elicit enthusiastic commitment from employees because it can significantly contribute to their overall satisfaction with their accomplishments in life.

In their book *The Progress Principle,* Harvard Business School Professor Teresa Amabile and psychologist Steven Kramer report on a long-term research project about understanding employee motivation. Consistent with the PCT view of human behavior in which meaningful progress at work is a high-level goal of employees, they note:

> Conventional management wisdom is way off track about employee psychology. When we surveyed hundreds of managers around the world, ranging from CEOs to project leaders, about what motivates employees, we found startling results: 95 percent of these leaders fundamentally misunderstood the most important source of motivation.

Our research inside companies revealed that the best way to motivate people, day in and day out, is by facilitating *progress*—even small wins. But the managers in our survey ranked "supporting progress" dead last as a work motivator.

… When you do what it takes to facilitate progress in work people care about, managing them—and managing the organization—becomes much more straightforward. You don't need to parse people's psyches or tinker with their incentives, because helping them succeed at making a difference virtually guarantees good inner work life *and* strong performance. It's more cost-effective than relying on massive incentives, too. When you don't manage for progress, no amount of emotional intelligence or incentive planning will save the day.[55]

In summary, the four core beliefs described in this chapter operate at a deeper cognitive level than the typical recommendations for improving management decision making. For example, it makes sense for management, as others have recommended, to focus on confirming or disconfirming, as quickly as possible, the key make-or-break assumption that underpins a new business venture. However, the improved worldview that is the topic of this chapter can help management discover in the first place exactly what that critical assumption actually is, as well as identify related assumptions that may now be obsolete. The next section illustrates how all four core beliefs can help you analyze a business situation.

Why Michelin's run-flat tires failed

In 2004, the consumer research firm J. D. Powers and Associates predicted that by 2010, 80 percent of new cars would be equipped with Michelin's innovative run-flat tires. With these new tires, a light would flash on the dashboard alerting you to a tire puncture. Instead of having a flat and being stranded on the side of the road, you could drive at normal speed for up to 125 miles to get to a tire-repair service center. By not having to carry a spare tire, the other benefits are increased trunk space and reduced vehicle weight. To management's surprise, Michelin's innovation led to an expensive write-off due to a lack of significant commercial adoption. Let's analyze why that happened, using the four core beliefs as the framework.

First, recall that past experience shapes assumptions. Michelin gained its top position in the tire industry due to its invention of the radial tire, which did, in fact, revolutionize the tire industry. From this experience, management was primed to believe that the run-flat tire invention that solved important customer needs would certainly also be a big commercial success, just like radial tires had been.

Second, it is easy to be unaware that language is perception's silent partner. Michelin management's language helped craft a future reality for them in which commercial success was assured. In management's words:

> ... our biggest technological breakthrough since we patented the radial tire in 1946 ... in single terms, we have reinvented the tire ... adoption of [run-flat tires] is inevitable ... we consider it a major development in vehicle safety, as important as the introduction of radials, if not more important ... they [run-flat tires] perform better in every respect. In ten years, there won't be any other kind of tire ...[56]

Third, a valuable guide for management is to improve performance by identifying and fixing a system's key constraints. Michelin management failed to use a comprehensive systems perspective, which would have pinpointed that the critical constraint to achieving success was the participation of the service centers that repair tires. The lack of convenient access to tire-repair service centers that were equipped to handle run-flat tires resulted in people having to buy expensive new tires, often in pairs to maintain vehicle alignment.

Fourth, understand people from the inside out because behavior is control of perception. If you want to predict how people will behave, figure out the key variables they are trying to control. Sometimes it is a difficult task to get a handle on the higher-order goals that matter most to people. In the case of the managers of tire-repair service centers, the clear answer was profitability. To repair run-flat tires, service centers would need to purchase expensive new equipment and also train their employees to pass Michelin's certification process. Importantly, sizable investments by service centers were upfront investments that would not provide meaningful cash flows for many years, i.e., until there was a significant number of cars on the road equipped with run-flat tires. Service center managers chose not to participate. Management's perceived inevitable success for run-flat tires turned into a major financial loss for Michelin.

CHAPTER 5

The Firm's Foundational Culture and Business Performance

When there's little competitive threat, when high profit margins and a commanding market position are assumed, then the economic and market forces that other companies have to live or die by simply don't apply. In that environment, what would you expect to happen? The company and its people lose touch with external realities, *because what's happening in the marketplace is essentially irrelevant to the success of the company.*

… This hermetically sealed quality—an institutional viewpoint that anything important [in the computer industry] started inside the company—was, I believe, the root cause of many of our problems … [leading to] a general disinterest in customer needs, accompanied by a preoccupation with internal politics. There was a general permission to stop projects dead in their tracks, a bureaucratic infrastructure that defended turf instead of promoting collaboration, and a management class that presided rather than acted. IBM even had a language all its own.

—Lou Gerstner[57]

IBM delivered peak profits in 1990. Three years later, Schumpeter's concept of creative destruction was tearing down IBM's bureaucratic organization at a rapid pace. Bankruptcy was on the horizon. IBM's new CEO, Lou Gerstner, orchestrated a remarkable turnaround. Later, he said, "… I came to see, in my time at IBM, that culture isn't just one aspect of the game. It *is* the game."

What is culture and why is it so important?

A worldview comprises your strongly held assumptions that operate at a high level in your own hierarchical control system (discussed in the previous chapter) and that automatically and silently influence your perceptions and behavior. Let's label that part of an employee's worldview relevant to how their firm functions as their business worldview. *A firm's foundational culture can then be defined as the aggregation of the business worldviews shared by management and all the employees of the firm.*

This definition of a firm's *foundational culture* is focused on the high-level, cognitive aspects of worldviews, including the extent to which the four core beliefs for improving worldviews are put into practice. For example, the core belief about systems thinking and identifying a system's key constraint is critically important both for small, startup firms as well as large, mature organizations. So, too, for the other core beliefs to improve business performance.

Definitions of culture that stress lower-level aspects of behavior will point to the need for cultural changes as a firm transitions over its life cycle.[58] From this viewpoint, when a firm has, say, 100 employees and expands to 100,000, the lower-level rules of behavior for new product development surely must change. Nevertheless, the importance of higher-order principles concerned with, for example, ethical behavior and knowledge building (questioning of assumptions, experimentation, and feedback) do not change as the firm grows larger. The life-cycle chart for 3M (Figure 2.3) is a striking example of wealth creation through management's constant focus on knowledge building and innovation.

Of course, management might talk and write about their firm's culture as being commendable, but their behavior can cause employees to disagree. In that case, the aggregation of business worldviews, heavily weighted by employees' unfavorable beliefs, produces a dysfunctional culture. Research has shown that advertised cultural values are unimportant. However, the level of integrity of management, as perceived by the employees, is shown to be a significant predictor of firm performance.[59]

One characteristic of IBM's dysfunctional culture was noted in Gerstner's opening quote, i.e., " ... viewpoint that anything important [in the computer industry] started inside the company." IBM management's business worldview significantly impaired their perception of changes taking place outside IBM, to the detriment of knowledge building. And that resonates with the scientific finding that our perception of the world "out there" is a function of how our brains work. Research using brain scans has documented that when people view video clips of political situations that are in conflict with their worldview, those components of the brain devoted to logic and reason go dormant.[60] Since worldviews are not easily changed, it follows that changing a firm's culture is a challenging task.

In the center of Figure 5.1 are four especially important components of management's worldview. These components are: the firm's vision (reason for being), its level of commitment to employees, its approach to the dual tasks of innovation and efficiency, and its expectations of ethical behavior. Management's core assumptions (stakes in the ground, true beliefs) about each component, their skill in communicating them, and how closely their own behavior corresponds to their stated core assumptions, ultimately determines the type of foundational culture that permeates the firm. Keep in mind that while the higher-order components of management's worldview remain unchanged, accepted rules of behavior for getting things done can change over time as the organization becomes more complex. As seen in this figure, the impact of management's worldview on culture varies from a dysfunctional culture to a high-performance one.

Figure 5.1: Dysfunctional culture versus high-performance culture

Dysfunctional Culture	Management's Worldview	High-Performance Culture
My work provides a paycheck, nothing more.	← Vision →	My work helps me live a purposeful life.
I don't trust management.	← Commitment to employees →	I trust management.
Avoid identifying problems and challenging people's thinking. Better to reduce accounting costs in small but fail-safe ways.	← Innovation and efficiency →	Experimentation and systematic problem solving is how we make progress.
Do whatever it takes to make accounting targets. Never "rat out" a coworker.	← Ethical behavior →	Ethical standards (including integrity) are nonnegotiable and a code of honor that we practice proudly.

The top priority for CEOs should be to develop and sustain a high-performance culture. How important is a CEO's use of language in shaping their firm's culture? Consider the contrasting leadership skills in communicating to employees of Jack Welsh, who as CEO of General Electric delivered solid performance, and Roger Smith, who as CEO of General Motors presided over a trajectory for GM that eventually led to bankruptcy.[61] In their shareholder letters, Welch described a new and better GE that was doable and inspirational, whereas Smith ignored GM's obvious problems and laid out a vision of the future that was disconnected from business realities. Smith tended to ignore GM's deteriorating performance, to assume that the future would mirror past successes, and to assert that GM's troubles were not related to any shortcomings with the internal management of the business, but rather, due to external forces. Here is a sample from GM's 1987 annual report:

> GM today is the leading car manufacturer in the world by a wide margin. We build and sell nearly one out of every five cars purchased in the entire free world. Precisely because of our great organizational and financial strengths, we have been able over recent years to transform GM into a 21st century corporation, so that we can be expected to grow even stronger and more profitable in the years ahead.

In contrast, Welch's decision making at GE was broadly consistent with his rhetoric. Welch often portrayed a vision for GE that was inspiring and aligned employees' higher-level goals for a productive life with work at GE. Here are two examples from the 1989 and 1990 GE annual reports:

> We want GE to become a company where people come to work every day in a rush to try something they woke up thinking about the night before. We want them to go home from work wanting to talk about what they did that day, rather than try and forget about it. We want factories where the whistle blows and everyone wonders where the time went, and someone suddenly wonders aloud why we need a whistle.
>
> "Boundaryless" is an uncommon word—perhaps even an awkward one—but it has become a word we use constantly, one that describes a whole set of behaviors we believe are necessary.... In a boundaryless company, suppliers aren't "outsiders." ... Customers are seen for what they are—the lifeblood of the company.... In a boundaryless company, internal functions begin to blur.... Even the

barriers between GE work life and community life have come down.

To sum up, there is a general consensus that during Jack Welch's tenure at GE the firm had a high-performance culture whereas Rodger Smith's leadership at GM resulted in a dysfunctional culture. Knowledge about a widely shared culture in an organization enables one to predict how its management perceives the world. Recall the prior discussion about how our brains are always seeking patterns and using assumptions to select incoming signals from the environment while filling in details, thereby creating our perception of the world "out there." Along this line of thought, Peter Senge told a story about a conversation he had with Detroit auto executives after their initial visit to Japan at the time when Japan was clearly beginning to take a significant share of the auto market. The U.S. executives were dismissive of the Japanese because they claimed that on the tour of Japanese plants they were not shown "real plants." To the U.S. executives, extraordinarily low inventories in Japanese plants were not possible at real plants—the kind of plants the executives were experienced in operating. However, in reality, the Toyota lean production system with just-in-time inventories was the source of the favorable reduction in inventories as well as a harbinger of major difficulties GM would face on its road to being what Rodger Smith then was extolling as a 21st century corporation.[62]

More on how to change a culture

In Chapter 4, human behavior was explained as our being wired as a hierarchical control system where what we value the most (high-level control variables) explains the actions we take in hopes that the consequences keep us in control. Employees want to work for management they can trust will deal with them fairly and respectfully. Working for management that is trusted is one of their most important, high-level goals. It is devastating to a firm's culture when employees don't trust management. Because then they tune out management's business goals and feel they are being exploited without any chance for a win–win relationship.[63]

Keep in mind the important point that past experiences shape assumptions. When many experiences consistently demonstrate that management is not to be trusted, employees conclude that it is no longer their provisional interpretation but, rather, that management *is truly untrustworthy.* That assumption—now an accepted belief—is not easily changed.

How can new management change such a belief and remake a currently dysfunctional culture? For new management to simply assert they are different and should be trusted will not work. What is needed are concrete new experiences that clearly demonstrate that new management consistently acts in ways that justifiably earns the trust of employees. A classic example of how such a cultural change was achieved is the Toyota–GM joint venture, automotive plant in Fremont, California.

It is an understatement to say that the Fremont plant was the worst-performing plant owned by GM. The employees routinely filed grievances as part of their workday; frequently went on strike; on occasion, sabotaged quality; regularly failed to show up for work with absenteeism at 20 percent; and the list goes on. To no surprise, GM cars earning the lowest quality rating were produced in that plant. The plant was shut down in 1982.[64]

In 1984, a company jointly owned by Toyota and GM—New United Motor Manufacturing, Inc. (NUMMI)—reopened the plant. Toyota was eager to gain its first manufacturing base in the U.S. as well as learn how to train U.S. workers. GM wanted to put an idle plant to work, get Toyota's help in producing a quality small car, and learn about the Toyota lean production system.

Of the new employees hired by Toyota, 85 percent had previously worked in the plant. However, Toyota was successful in transferring its culture of teamwork and mutual trust to those very same unionized employees who had previously worked there. Remarkably, within just a year NUMMI became GM's best-performing plant with top-of-the-chart quality ratings for its cars. A unique window to understand how this happened was offered by John Shook, CEO of the Lean Enterprise Institute. Prior to the formation of NUMMI, he was the first American hired by Toyota in Japan, and he subsequently played a pivotal role in the cultural transformation at NUMMI.

Shook emphasized how Toyota focused on changing how employees did their work. NUMMI employees learned about Toyota's "Respect for People," i.e., a commitment to support employees in standardizing work, uncovering problems, and systematically fixing the root causes of problems. In this way, Toyota committed to helping employees succeed in making quality an integral part of the production process. Employees responded enthusiastically to being given the opportunity to excel in their jobs and to continually experience that management fulfills their commitments with training, tools, and mentoring.

For employees, this was a new world. In the old world, a good way to get fired was to stop the line even when serious defects (e.g., defective brake assemblies) were observed. In the new world, employees had an obligation to notify their team leader immediately on seeing a problem, which might then result in stopping the line (pulling the andon cord). American supervisors uniformly acknowledged, after completing training sessions in Japan, *the unique value of finding and solving problems without blaming anyone.* Shook tells the story of Susumu Uchikawa, a Toyota production control manager, who would explain to American supervisors that he did not want to hear "No problem" when they were asked about production. Uchikawa would reply, "No problem is problem! Managers' job is to see problems!" Such a radically different way of working enabled NUMMI employees to quickly *experience* the satisfaction and pride of belonging to a team that produced an exceptionally high-quality product.[65]

As part of securing a win–win relationship with employees, Toyota made a remarkable (from the perspective of the United Auto Workers union) commitment in the union contract. For Toyota, continual productivity improvements required the elimination of the onerous job classification restrictions that were a standard component of union contracts. The union agreed, and in return Toyota agreed that, in difficult times, management salaries would be cut first. Then, previously outsourced work would be pulled back into the plant. Only as a last resort would employee layoffs be considered. In NUMMI's second year of operation, consumers' tastes turned to cars other than Chevy Novas, which were then being manufactured in the plant. Sales plummeted 30 percent below planned production levels. There were no layoffs. Toyota increased training programs and quickly moved production of Toyota Corollas to the Fremont plant. Through concrete experiences, NUMMI employees learned to trust management.

It was not so easy to achieve a similar cultural transformation across all GM plants. When Jack Smith became GM's CEO in 1992, he soon placed NUMMI alumni throughout GM and made some progress, yet the bureaucratic inefficiencies in the company were too widespread. During the 2008/2009 recession, GM's financial problems accelerated and NUMMI was abandoned. In 2010, we once again could observe Schumpeter's creative destruction at work when Tesla Motors purchased the plant from GM.

Toyota Kata

Mike Rother, author of *Toyota Kata: Managing People for Improvement, Adaptiveness, and Superior Results*, has extensively studied Toyota manufacturing plants. His research applied Toyota-type practices in non-Toyota plants, and he analyzed in detail what did not work. His primary research question was, Why do firms that copy Toyota's highly visible lean tools, such as value stream mapping, takt time, andon, kanban, and the like, invariably fail to match Toyota's productivity? Rother's analysis focused on how Toyota manages people in order to *routinely* improve and adapt. For the most part, Toyota imitators do not match Toyota's organizational routines for continuous process improvement and adaptation, which is aided by not being distracted by having to deliver specified accounting-based results. In other words, improve the process and the accounting results will follow.

Rother focused on how management uses the concept of *kata* as an integral part of how work is done. Kata is a pattern of thinking and behaving that becomes so automatic it is not immediately visible to outside observers. Recall the Chapter 4 discussion of Perceptual Control Theory with its emphasis on how high-level control variables (goals) are not visible to those observing a person's behavior. But these goals ultimately determine behavior. Kata operates at a high level in one's hierarchical control system and is central to Toyota culture.

Previously, a knowledge-building culture was listed as one of management's core responsibilities. Further, the knowledge-building process was described as a loop of interrelated components: knowledge base, purposes, worldview, perceptions, actions and their consequences, and feedback—all of which are influenced by language. These interconnected components (see Figure 4.1) were illustrated in the overview presented of Edward Jenner's development of an effective vaccine for smallpox. These components have a general applicability to help us understand how knowledge is built up. The same components are used below to review Rother's analysis of the role of kata in Toyota's knowledge-building culture.

KNOWLEDGE BASE

Many businesspeople are sure that uncertainty necessitates planning. Most often this involves Excel spreadsheets and forecast scenarios. And the higher in the firm one goes, the more reasonable this assumption seems. But improving businesses processes, i.e., where the work is actually done, is all about experimenting in order to deal with uncertainty as it arises. The path from a current condition to a target condition (what Rother labels the gray zone) *cannot* be planned in advance. Navigating the gray zone requires a building up of one's knowledge base by testing hypotheses and, based on what was learned, adapting and moving forward.

PURPOSES

Toyota employees focus on target conditions, which amounts to the specified purpose of where they want to be. How to get there is initially uncertain. Of course, there are always a multitude of actions we can take that might incrementally improve a process, and people always seem to have their favorite choices. But target conditions narrow the choices and help employees to identify and test the most viable ways to move forward.

WORLDVIEW

A foundational part of Toyota management's worldview is the strong belief that processes are either improving or deteriorating. Left alone, the natural tendency is for workarounds and ill-conceived quick "fixes" to creep into a process. But it is continual improvement that is essential.

Management is fundamentally about instilling the best procedures to build knowledge. When employees are confident about *how* to deal with uncertainty, they are prepared to continually improve within a *changing* environment.

From a broad systems perspective, Toyota management is keenly aware of how maximizing local efficiencies (e.g., install faster machines) can, at times, be counterproductive to improving the efficiency of the overall system. Management favors process improvements that facilitate uninterrupted flow with a minimum of waste.

In the following quote, Rother's comments resonate with the ideas in Chapter 4 for improving worldviews:

... there is a human tendency to desire and even artificially create a sense of certainty. It is conceivable that the point here is not that we do not see the problems in our processes, but rather that we do not *want* to see them because that would undermine the sense of certainty we have about how our factory is working. It would mean that some of our assumptions, some things we have worked for and are attached to, may not be true.

... Toyota's improvement kata involves teaching people a standardized conscious "means" for sensing the gist of situations and responding scientifically. This is a different way for humans to have a sense of security, comfort, and confidence. Instead of obtaining that from an unrealistic sense of certainty about conditions, they get it from the means by which they deal with uncertainty. This channels and taps our capabilities as humans much better than our current management approach, explains a good deal of Toyota's success, and gives us a model for managing almost any human enterprise.[66]

PERCEPTIONS

An enormously significant issue is that it is typical of many business cultures to *perceive problems as failures*. This is a major roadblock to achieving a high-performance culture. Rother explains it this way:

... the improvement kata should be depersonalized and have a positive, challenging, no-blame feeling. Toward that end, at Toyota an abnormality or problem is generally not thought of or judged good or bad, but as an occurrence that may teach us something about our work system. This can be somewhat difficult for westerners to understand: something can be a problem—a situation that we do not want—without it necessarily being considered good or bad. This is akin to the difference between "understanding" and "accepting." Trying to understand a situation and why it happens does not mean you have to accept it. Making this distinction will make you a better problem solver.[67]

ACTIONS AND CONSEQUENCES

There is a difference between a target and a target condition. Language matters. Rother explains that a target is an outcome, whereas a *target condition is the way a process operates to produce the desired outcome.* As previously noted, there are always a variety of actions that might yield a desired consequence. This variety has the potential to offer up quick solutions that "seem right," but lack rigorous evidence. Within a Toyota culture, there is a pattern of *scientific thinking* attuned to revealing root problems and generating empirical evidence to guide solutions to these problems. For example, a target of reduced inventories by itself can be achieved in ways that are actually detrimental to overall efficiency. This situation easily results when accounting-based EVA targets are imposed on operating levels in the firm without regard for how process improvements are made.

FEEDBACK

Feedback that merely specifies outcomes is of little help to learning. Toyota's improvement kata provides detailed feedback at each step along the journey to reach a target condition. Finding a problem and solving it changes the process. All the more reason to quickly gain feedback as to what is learned in the next step. So, by focusing on a single problem and a single countermeasure, feedback about actual results compared to expected ones is more reliable than having multiple problems being investigated simultaneously. In operation, the improvement kata is based on fast feedback and primarily involves team leaders and supervisors. All employees have a mentor who gives feedback (advice) to them as part of doing actual assigned work.

To sum up, a culture like Toyota's that is focused on experimentation and problem solving is the polar opposite of a culture that rewards managers for their "skill" at firefighting and workarounds to achieve short-term accounting results.

Cleveland Clinic

Since every system has a goal, changes to processes in the system should be designed to improve performance in achieving the overall system goal. Change falls into two broad categories. First is to strive for continual improvement as an integral part of how employees work, e.g., the Toyota kata culture. Second is to locate the system's key constraints and focus management's attention and resources on fixing these bottlenecks. At times, a firm's way of "how we do things around here" (the firm's culture) involves an entrenched, obsolete assumption that needs to be purged in order to fix the constraint that holds back performance. So, how might systems thinking and cultural change be applied to improving the delivery of healthcare in hospitals, for example?

In a typical hospital, many physicians are independent contractors who bring customers (patients) to the hospital for treatment such as surgery. Seriously ill patients, in particular, spend a great deal of time connecting with various doctors and undergoing myriad tests—all in a distinctly noncentralized manner. As independent contractors, physicians have a financial incentive to focus on more profitable treatments and to order medical tests that might not be needed but would be helpful in defending against a potential malpractice lawsuit. Those of us with patient experiences in hospitals could continue to list ways that patients are disappointed (or injured) due to a lack of high-quality care.

It is worthwhile to look at one hospital organization that changed its culture in very smart ways for the benefit of its patients. In 2004, Dr. Delos M. Cosgrove became CEO of the Cleveland Clinic, a nonprofit multispecialty academic hospital complex in Cleveland, Ohio, which is part of a larger health organization with 43,000 employees. Before he became CEO, Cosgrove was a preeminent cardiac surgeon at the Cleveland Clinic and was well known for his successful innovations in improving clinical outcomes for heart surgery. For decades, the Cleveland Clinic was highly rated across many specialties for its clinical outcomes. And Cosgrove's surgical skills were symbolic of that technical excellence. However, the organization was noted for poor performance in taking care of patients before and after surgery. Feedback to Cosgrove was that the organization lacked empathy.

Keep in mind that motivated, creative people can produce an excellent patient experience in an inefficient way by exceptional effort and working around bottlenecks. But the systems approach is the path forward to achieve continuous improvement, reduce waste, lower overall costs, and achieve excellent patient experiences as a normal outcome. The Cleveland Clinic is organized differently than most hospital enterprises in ways that show an appreciation for systems thinking in order to achieve the goal of a high-quality, overall patient experience in the most efficient (cost-effective) manner. It is a physician-run organization, which ensures that policies are rooted in the patients' best interest. All physicians are paid a salary and are part of a group practice. By eliminating independent-contractor physicians, everyone is on the same team. This facilitates collaboration and system-wide changes to improve processes while avoiding the trap of improving local efficiencies (and dealing with related turf battles) that do not translate into overall system efficiency gains. Moreover, in a group practice physicians can be much more focused on patient care since all the administrative burdens of running a business are eliminated. They are also free to not worry about malpractice claims that could devastate an independent-contractor physician. And that freedom translates into taking actions that are solely in the patients' best interests. Cosgrove noted:

> In 2010, we gathered together every caregiver involved in lung transplantation for a step-by-step analysis of our lung transplant program to see if we could get even better results by improving teamwork. We streamlined processes, eliminated redundant tasks, and pared every last bit of procedural fat.… not only were patients getting home faster, but they were living longer.… Imagine replicating that plan across specialties, with similar medical outcomes—from how epilepsy patients are cared for to how babies are delivered to how patients who need prostate surgery are treated. As a culture of continuous improvement begins to take shape, the hospital becomes a very different place.[68]

Cosgrove further noted their adoption of a lean, Toyota-style kata culture with emphasis on target conditions:

> To promote ongoing cost awareness and savings, we created scorecards that quantify and measure quality and cost, and we set goals: "Cut costs on heart valve implants by 20 percent while improving quality by 10 percent." … Adopting this approach in a conventional setting would be difficult because the doctors all work for different organizations with different bottom lines. In a group practice, it's considerably easier.[69]

The Cleveland Clinic's extreme focus on collaboration and teamwork is particularly helpful when their patients have complications, because a top-notch specialist with expertise in dealing with the particular complication is readily available. Based on his experience in developing breakthrough innovations in heart surgery, Cosgrove orchestrates collaboration to promote creativity at the boundaries among disciplines. Note how insights derived from collaboration across the entire care-giving system could not be obtained if attention were focused solely on individual components of the system.

To further spur teamwork and collaboration while centralizing care for patients, the Cleveland Clinic founded institutes focused on specific diseases or organ systems—institutes organized from the patients' perspective as opposed to the conventional way where doctors group themselves by medical specialty. With institutes, patients walk into a building that houses all the medical specialists they might need. This centralized physical layout favorably affects the care path of patients while facilitating continuous process improvements.

In addition to all these improvements, the Cleveland Clinic is a leader in utilizing electronic medical records. It gains efficiency in the use of data due to standardized procedures across the entire health care system. Over a three-year period beginning in 2009, the incidence of IV tube infections was cut 75 percent after analyzing data to identify the causes of the problem and guide the creation of new protocols.

To sum up, a patient's total experience consists of a clinical experience, a physical experience, and an emotional experience. After being appointed CEO, Cosgrove concluded that criticism about the organization's lack of empathy was valid. It was consistent with the emotional experiences of patients being rated far below their high-quality clinical experiences. He then staked out a vision to efficiently deliver exceptional high-quality, total patient experiences. The purpose of that vision is to clearly communicate the reason why employees should be enthusiastic about coming to work every day. He condensed the vision into this motto: "Patients First." To this day employees wear "Patients First" lapel pins—a simple, yet powerful, motto that guides organizational alignment and was a step forward toward an improved culture.

Dr. James Merlino, Chief Experience Officer at the Cleveland Clinic, was instrumental in implementing Cosgrove's vision. Merlino emphasizes that a health care organization must not have one standard of behavior for doctors and a different standard for everyone else. So everyone from doctors to parking lot attendants is called a caregiver, consistent with the vision. Merlino warns against announcing that a culture is now going to change. Rather, he says it is better to describe where the organization is and where management wants it to be.[70] The Cleveland Clinic is widely acknowledged as the model for other health organizations to follow for the benefit of patients, and also for the benefit of society in having resources efficiently used to deliver high value in health care.

Culture, life-cycle reality, and strategy

Chapter 1 noted how Whole Foods Market's John Mackey, over the course of his business career, came to understand and enthusiastically embrace the societal benefits of voluntary exchange and competition. As previously noted, Mackey stated that "… the value created by the business will be divided among the creators of the value approximately equal to the contribution each market participant made." As such, his worldview, rooted in win–win partnerships, shaped the firm's culture and is reflected in the firm's vision:

> Whole Foods Market is a dynamic leader in the quality food business. We are a mission-driven company that aims to set the standards of excellence for food retailers. We are building a business in which high standards permeate all aspects of our company. Quality is a state of mind at Whole Foods Market.
>
> Our motto—Whole Foods, Whole People, Whole Planet—emphasizes that our vision reaches far beyond just

being a food retailer. Our success in fulfilling our vision is measured by customer satisfaction, team member happiness and excellence, return on capital investment, improvement in the state of the environment and local and larger community support.[71]

Over the years, Whole Foods management's behavior has been consistent with this vision. To no surprise, employees have embraced this vision. The firm's life-cycle track record is displayed in Figure 5.2.

Whole Foods was the pioneer in selling exceptionally high-quality, healthy food with a minimum of artificial additives, including organically grown food. The top panel in the figure shows that Whole Foods has earned the cost of capital or higher from 1991 to 2014. The middle panel shows extraordinary asset growth during the 1990s and then trending lower. The bottom panel shows that Whole Foods' stock has outperformed the market over the long term, although a falloff in economic returns during the 2008/2009 recession caused a substantial underperformance. Let's focus on the very high asset growth rates in the early years. These growth rates far exceeded growth from only using internally generated cash flow (the source for organic growth). To implement its vision, management acquired many firms in the fragmented health foods industry, including Fresh Fields with its 22 stores. Then in 2007, they acquired their main competitor, Wild Oats Markets.

What is a plausible forecast for the future life cycle of Whole Foods? As of this writing, market expectations (explained in Chapter 6) are for future economic returns to approximate 6 percent real, which is the long-term corporate average, or cost of capital. This would place Whole Foods at the mature stage (see Figure 2.1) of its life cycle. Apparently, investors are concerned about heightened competition that offers similar high-quality food at the same or lower prices and view Whole Foods' competitive moat as shallow.

Figure 5.2: Whole Foods Market

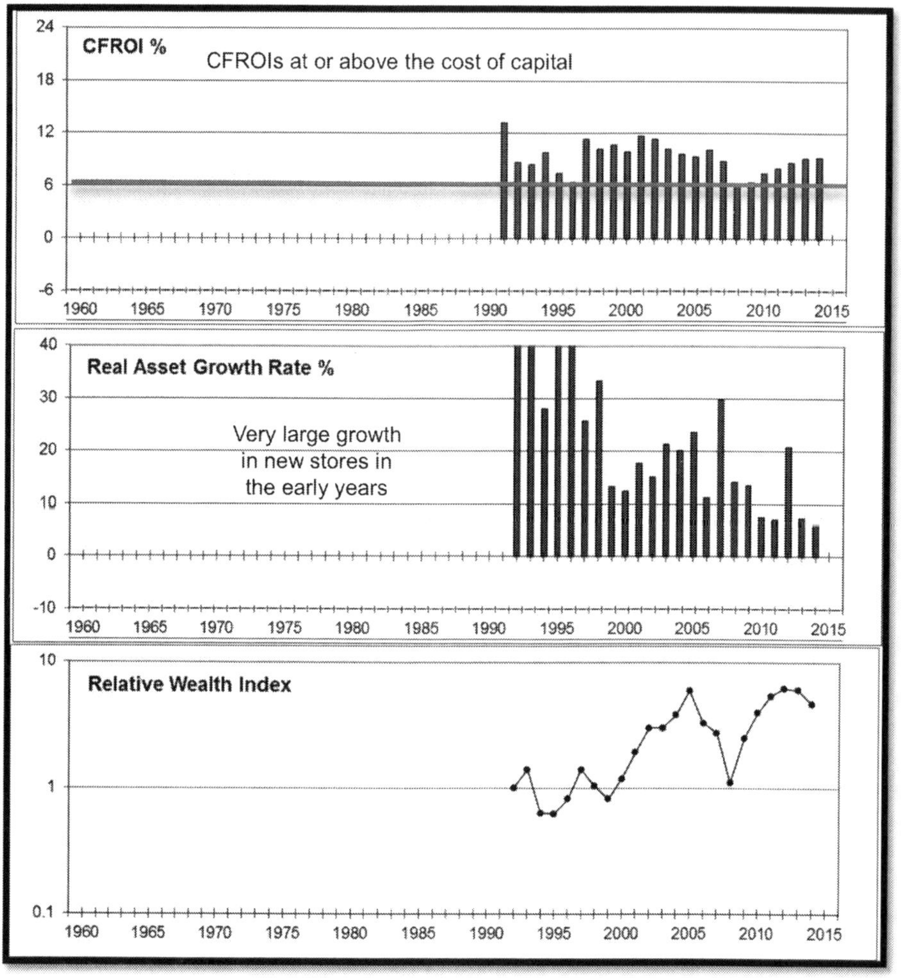

Source: Credit Suisse HOLT global database

Management's past success in becoming the dominant healthy food retailer was achieved through aggressive expansion via acquisitions. Consequently, there is a risk that "bigger is always better" might have become a strongly held assumption by management. From a life-cycle perspective, an alternative strategy is that the firm should focus primarily on earning economic returns above the cost of capital. This suggests that an emphasis on efficiency gains from existing assets should be the top priority, while experimenting on a small scale with new business opportunities. This would imply more modest asset growth rates (reinvestment rates) in the future, consistent with the following life-cycle performance objective summarized in Figure 3.3:

- Economic returns above the cost of capital, and
- reinvestment rates supportive of maintaining a
- favorable long-term fade rate.

Can America sustain a culture supportive of free-market capitalism?

Most managements would agree with the following proposition: If the firm is to get one thing right, get culture right. Because if a firm's culture is dysfunctional, the firm is guaranteed to encounter serious problems that can even threaten its very survival.

If culture is so important within firms, should it not be critically important as well for the environment in which firms operate? From a systems view, let's move up a level and see firms within the context of a society made up of people who do not support the principles of free-market capitalism. In that culture, a level playing field for competition, including freedom to enter new businesses, has been replaced with a heavily regulated environment that favors large incumbents, especially those with powerful lobbies and friends in Washington. Resource allocation decisions are influenced less and less by the marketplace and increasingly by laws and regulations handed down from Washington. Welcome to the new culture that is fast gaining hold in the United States. Disagree? Try starting up a new community bank and dealing with the requirements of the 2,300-page Dodd-Frank financial legislation of 2010 that clearly favors already existing large financial institutions whose lobbyists actually helped craft the legislation. That is but one example.

This is not an abstract argument. To quantify what is happening, refer to the Fraser Institute's annual assessment of economic freedom, freetheworld.com, which covers five critical areas:

- Size of government (e.g., expenditures and taxes)
- Legal structure and security of property rights
- Access to sound money
- Freedom to trade internationally
- Regulation of credit, labor, and business

In the year 2000, the United States was ranked second out of all countries for economic freedom, behind Hong Kong and Singapore, which were tied for first place. By 2013, the U.S. had dropped in rank to 16th out of 157 countries for economic freedom. The universe of countries includes many small ones, some of which are disasters for freedom of any kind for their citizens (e.g., Angola, Zimbabwe). Current data puts countries such as New Zealand, Switzerland, Ireland, Canada, and Chile well ahead of the United States. Extensive research has found that countries with a culture that supports freedom tend to: reinvest at higher rates, deliver faster economic growth, produce higher income levels, and show faster declines in poverty. We need to reverse the U.S. trend of losing economic freedom. Let's consider the role of corporate managements (and boards of directors that oversee management) and how they contribute to our changing culture.

Most CEOs of large corporations are likely to agree that the cultural shift away from free-market capitalism is a very serious problem that needs to be fixed. However, a good bet is that they would also say that the task of shaping our society's culture is not a task for them. In a sense, we are dealing with a system in which those responsible for system components (individual firms) are focused on maximizing local efficiencies (firms' near-term profits) without regard for the health of the overall system (the long-term well-being of all members of the society). From the perspective of local efficiency, lobbying in Washington for tax breaks, tariffs, government loan guarantees, and such is appealing, as it can boost near-term profits and hurt potential competitors. But ideally the system's components should be managed with an eye toward achieving the system goal of prosperity for all. Probably the most expeditious way to sharply reduce crony capitalism is through educating American voters, who could then elect politicians who are committed to free-market principles. Meanwhile, consider how a firm might perform with highly skilled leadership that is totally committed to free-market capitalism and makes extraordinary efforts to shape the firm's culture along these lines. That would be Koch Industries.

Koch Industries

Charles Koch joined Koch Industries in 1961, a time when this small, oil-gathering firm had sales less than $2 million. A few years later he became CEO and under his leadership the firm has grown to 100,000 employees today in diverse industrial businesses with an estimated 2014 market value of approximately $100 billion. The culture at Koch Industries has evolved over time to reflect the strongly held beliefs of Charles Koch that are based on a rigorous continual learning process. His book *Good Profit: How Creating Value for Others Built One of the World's Most Successful Companies* offers a unique way to understand this cultural evolution. Koch explains his successes and failures, including his intellectual journey to deeply understand the wide disparity in progress of different societies over time and how this knowledge applies to the management of business enterprise.

Charles Koch is an independent thinker with a scientific mindset and a high-energy curiosity for discovering management practices that accelerate wealth creation. At the macro level of societies, his early research reaffirmed the fundamental role of free-market capitalism in furthering

economic progress. He concluded that these macro-wealth-creation principles should not only guide the management of Koch Industries but also
become the strongly held beliefs of every Koch employee (similar to John
Allison's management style at BB&T, discussed in Chapter 1). Within
such a culture, management doesn't need to tightly control employees'
behavior. Because management and employees share the same high-level
goals, employees themselves have the freedom to figure out what to do to
create long-term value. Koch summarizes his views as follows:

> Good profit comes from … creating superior value for our
> customers while consuming fewer resources and always
> acting lawfully and with integrity … we earn profits by cre-
> ating value—for customers, society, our partners, and every
> employee who contributes.
>
> Too often, Washington chooses winners and losers in
> the economy. This is corporate welfare, and it's the opposite
> of freedom and good profit. I have spent a lot of energy and
> resources speaking out about the dangers of profit by coer-
> cion, which is the antithesis of our Market-Based Manage-
> ment (MBM) philosophy.
>
> Market-Based Management emphasizes Principled Entre-
> preneurship over corporate welfare, virtue over talent, chal-
> lenge over hierarchy, comparative advantage over job title,
> and rewards for long-term value creation over managing to
> budgets. MBM has enabled Koch to spread well-being to our
> employees, to all those who benefit from our products and
> services, *and* to all those who benefit from the resources con-
> served by our greater efficiency and creativity.[72]

Market-Based Management is a fundamental way of thinking and acting that is an integral part of the firm's foundational culture.

Vision

The firm's overarching vision is to earn good profit by efficiently providing products and services valued by customers. This is about value creation and people—both customers and Koch employees. By stressing a continual development of firm capabilities, management is not committed to any specific industries. A concern for building new capabilities is consistent with Jeff Bezos' approach at Amazon (discussed in Chapter 3). A focus on adaptability and nurturing new capabilities is critical to large organizations to be able to beat the fade and achieve sustained high economic returns and high reinvestment rates in spite of their big size. On the flip side, Koch management is willing to exit a business when its life-cycle position implies limited opportunities for Koch to earn economic returns substantially more than the cost of capital.

Virtue and talents

The firm hires first based on a judgment of a person's values and then considers their talents. This is critical to maintaining a culture of non-negotiable, high ethical standards. Recall in Chapter 1 how BB&T front-line managers recommended to top management to forego profits from selling negative amortization loans because they believed these loans would eventually harm their customers (and they were right). And BB&T weathered the 2007/2008 financial crisis far better than its competitors, some of whom needed government bailouts.

For a culture professing high ethical standards to be embraced by employees, they must know that the standards apply to everyone in an unambiguous, hard-nosed fashion. Koch industries fired an environmental engineer in 1995 who falsified a report about a refinery's waste stream. Management did the right thing, which is not the easy thing to do, and voluntarily disclosed their awareness of the falsified report to the state environmental agency and then took corrective action. Not all firms behave this way.

One kind of dysfunctional culture buries unethical behavior. And often, as depicted in Figure 5.1, employees learn not to "rat out" a fellow employee who covers up an ethical breach. In this manner, employees come to expect similar treatment for their own misdeeds. This way of operating eventually goes bad. A prime example is GM's cover-up of a faulty ignition switch that could cut off power to a car's brakes, steering, and air bags. GM was hit with a $900 million fine in 2015. Much worse, coupled with over a decade-long cover-up, at least 124 occupants of GM cars were killed due to this faulty design. "While nothing can bring my daughter back, we need a system where auto executives are accountable to the public and not just corporate profits," said Laura Christian, whose 16-year-old daughter died in 2005 due to a faulty GM ignition switch.[73]

Knowledge processes

A hallmark of Koch Industries' culture is respect for getting better answers to problems and eliminating roadblocks from bureaucratic hierarchies that dampen debate and minimize creative thinking. Management nurtures an environment in which employees are invited to challenge assumptions. This type of constructive skepticism is especially healthy for a business organization and makes for faster and more productive cycles through the knowledge-building loop illustrated in Figure 4.1. Koch employees are encouraged to transition their ideas/hunches into testable hypotheses similar to how designers build fast prototypes to quickly generate concrete feedback and fast learning. Koch management learned to design experiments with full awareness of the magnitude of the risks involved.

Decision rights

Market-Based Management is all about enabling employees to have the freedom to figure out how best to create value. But to make their freedom operationally useful requires that employees' skill sets are a good match for their job responsibilities and that they "own" the decision rights in their area of responsibility. This is a two-way street in that their freedom entails responsibility for producing results. Employees have to be on the same page with management about making continual adjustments in decision rights in order to handle fast-paced innovation.

Incentives

To put employees on a path that boosts their creativity and maximizes their contributions, Koch employees are able to earn higher compensation than even their bosses. The idea is to purge budget-based compensation arrangements wedded to job titles. Instead, focus on the value created by individuals. Employees are paid a portion of the value they create for Koch Industries. Consistent with Charles Koch's commitment to free-market capitalism, there is no cap on what employees can earn.

To summarize, Koch Industries is a unique reflection of Charles Koch's own intellectual journey and perseverance in shaping a culture rooted in freedom, value to customers, efficiency and innovation, and respect for societal benefits to be gained from a level competitive playing field.

PART III:
THE FIRM'S PERFORMANCE AND VALUATION

CHAPTER 6

Valuation insights, Life-Cycle Reviews, and Integrated Reporting

[T]he mindset of boards must move from one of careful review to one of insatiable curiosity. … Question assumptions…. Boards should take personal responsibility for understanding how traditional budget processes and stretch goals frequently inculcate a lack of integrity in an organization and destroy value…. Rarely do board members have the kind of information they need to assess accurately the progress of the corporation. Getting that information requires boards to overhaul the process by which they get substantive information about corporate performance from one controlled by the CEO to one in which the board has ready access to relevant information.

—Michael C. Jensen and Joe Fuller[74]

In our opinion, outside pressures too often tempt companies to sacrifice long-term opportunities to meet quarterly market expectations…. If opportunities arise that might cause us to sacrifice short-term results but are in the best long-term interests of our

[Google] shareholders, we will take these opportunities.... We
would request that our shareholders take the long-term view.
—Larry Paige and Sergey Brin[75]

When a wildlife research biologist takes a walk in the countryside with someone lacking expertise in biology, the research biologist perceives the world differently than the companion. The biologist has specialized knowledge that explains phenomena in a fundamental way. For example, since birds eat moths, moths have evolved a dark brown color to blend in with trees. And so on. In this chapter, knowledge about the life-cycle valuation model is explained so as to provide a similar insightful understanding of stock prices. The point of this example is that a useful theory or model enables you to see the world differently and understand phenomena to a far greater degree. It enables you to get beyond surface knowledge and deal with cause-and-effect variables.

Both levels and changes in stock prices are important to understand

Clear thinking about wealth creation necessitates that managements and boards base their decision making on a logically sound and operationally useful valuation model. How is value created by the firm connected to its stock prices? This important question is answered in this chapter, with more technical details covered in Chapter 7. This chapter deals with the life-cycle valuation model, which applies the principles of discounted cash flow to determine the present value of firms' anticipated net cash receipts in the future.

First, let's examine some trends that have dampened academic interest in researching more robust ways to understand *levels* of firms' market values as opposed to short-term *changes* in their stock prices. Since the 1970s, mainstream finance has produced mountains of research articles about the efficiency of the market-pricing process in quickly assimilating value-relevant, public information. More recently, behavioral finance proponents have produced extensive findings showing that inefficiencies do exist in the market-pricing process. The efficient market proponents and the behavioral finance proponents do not need valuation models since their empirical focus is on changes in stock prices, not the level of firms' stock market valuations.

Meanwhile, intangible assets have been increasingly growing in importance so that equity market values have become disconnected from firms' book value (common equity). There is a widespread belief that the New Economy, driven by intangible (human capital) assets, has made valuation models much less useful because these models are perceived as ill-equipped to handle intangible assets.[76]

Finally, management has experienced increasing pressure to meet or beat Wall Street's quarterly earnings expectations. This hyperfocus on the short-term results in the following "model" being adopted—the bigger the favorable quarterly earnings surprise, the bigger the short-term rise in stock price, and vice versa. Using this guidepost, management decisions are then geared to do whatever it takes to produce quarterly accounting results that beat Wall Street's expectations—and this is not a good model.

From the perspective of management and boards, the ongoing efficient market/behavioral finance debate seems unrelated to major corporate decision making. Later in this chapter reasons are presented for much-needed improved communication among management, boards, and investors, including a proposed *Life-Cycle Review* not only to improve communication but also to improve board-level decisions. This opens up a fertile area for academic research to complement firms' financial staffs in connecting accounting-based performance, intangibles, and value creation—a task of high practical value.

As for quarterly reports, there is useful information for investors in these reports that differs from the extreme focus often put on beating a single earnings target. That is, a valuation model can be used to quantify long-term expectations in current market prices. And investors can then compare market expectations to their forecasted long-term scenarios. Then, investors can judge a firm's operating performance, investment outlays, and management's discussion of key issues within the context of long-term expectations. That is a sensible way to use quarterly data.

As to what drives long-term outperformance in the stock market, notice in Figure 6.1, which displays monthly stock prices for Walmart, that its stock price outperformed the S&P 500 Index 13-fold from 1980 to 1990.

Figure 6.1: Walmart versus the S&P 500 Index, 1980 to 2000

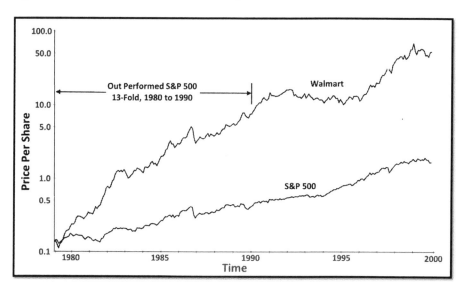

In the sections that follow, the life-cycle valuation model is described and used to explain what really caused Walmart's impressive stock market outperformance in the 1980s.

Net cash receipts

Although there are bubbles and crashes in stock markets, on average and over long time periods, stock prices do represent astute forecasts of firms' future prospects. So, what exactly is being forecasted?

Whether valuing stocks or bonds, economic logic and common sense leads to the conclusion that investors are concerned with *expected net cash receipts (NCRs)*. Expected NCRs for bonds are easy to forecast—interest and principal payments. However, it is not so easy to forecast NCRs for business firms.

To deal with this problem, a useful perspective for analyzing firms is that of the capital owners—equity and debt. The value of the equity is the total value of the firm less the value of its debt. NCRs for the total firm consist of after-tax cash inflows less investment outflows for maintaining existing assets and for new investments. Simply put, NCRs are what you get (cash inflows) less what you need to give up (cash outflows) along the way.

Forecasting NCRs is greatly helped by using the timeless life-cycle principles discussed in Chapter 2. Which is to say, above-average management skill can produce economic returns in excess of the cost of capital, yet competition is relentless in fading those returns toward the cost of capital over the long term. Before describing the link between valuation and life-cycle variables, it is useful first to work through a simplified example of a firm that illustrates important conceptual issues about NCRs and valuation. To keep the calculations straightforward, single-point estimates of NCRs are used (not a range of optimistic-to-pessimistic NCR scenarios).

Those readers well-versed in finance certainly do not need the present value (PV) mathematical explanation that is part of the valuation example in Figure 6.2. But they should be interested in the more technical valuation issues covered in Chapter 7. For the example below assume that investors demand a 5 percent per year return for investing in our sample firm and that NCRs from existing assets are $100 each year over a two-year life for the firm. To convert these NCRs to a present value today, we need PV factors. Since $1.00 today can grow to $1.05 at the demanded 5 percent return (the investors' discount rate), a dollar received a year hence is worth $1.00 x PV factor and the PV factor is 1.00/1.05 or 0.9524. Consequently, $100 NCR +1 year has a PV today of $100 x 0.9524 or $95.24, as shown in Figure 6.2. Repeating this process for +2 year and adding up the present values gives a value of $185.94 for existing assets.

Figure 6.2: Valuation of a firm

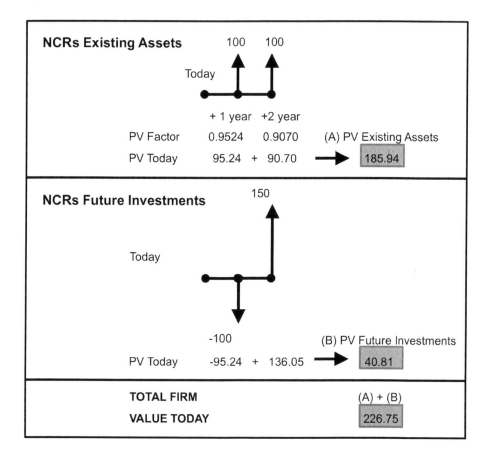

Further assume that management has announced a planned expenditure for a new, one-year-life investment for +1 year that will consume the $100 NCR generated from existing assets. Investors are aware of management's demonstrated skill and anticipate a 50 percent ROI (return-on-investment) on the $100, thereby providing a $150 NCR at +2 year. A similar PV exercise shows that the PV today of that future investment is $40.81. This is a *positive* and substantial amount because the ROI of 50 percent greatly exceeds the investors' discount rate of 5 percent. If the ROI were less than 5 percent, the value of future investments would have been *negative*.[77] The total value of the firm is $226.75 as the sum of $185.94 for existing assets plus $40.81 for future investments.

This exercise highlights how stock market valuations are attuned to ROIs on new investments. *All else being equal, the more capital reinvested in the future that achieves ROIs greater than the opportunity cost of capital, the higher the firm's market value.* Consequently, the middle panel of the life-cycle charts, which displays reinvestment rates (approximated by real asset growth rates), is especially important for high CFROI firms.

A firm's management, board, and shareholders should understand what a current stock price implies for the firm's future investments in order to better judge the economic soundness of management's planned capital expenditures. Business as usual is typically not strategically sound for firms priced with significant negative values for future investments.

In summary, the plain fact is that market prices are set by investors who make long-term forecasts of NCR streams. It is a mistake to conclude that short-term changes in stock prices around quarterly announcements imply a market pricing mechanism that disregards long-term forecasts. The long-term nature of stock prices becomes apparent the more one works with actual data using the life-cycle valuation model described below.

Components of the life-cycle valuation model

A valuation model is a mechanism to generate an expected long-term NCR stream for the firm and then translate this into a present value. Why not simply specify each year's NCR over the long term? This would result in users of the model then having no benchmarks to gauge the plausibility of the specified NCRs, especially those in the distant future. *The important point is that the valuation model should be constructed in a way that optimizes the use of historical firm data to help users improve their plausibility judgments about the inputs to the model.* The valuation model should facilitate a learning process, and not just be a logically sound application of discounted cash flow mathematics.

With a learning process in mind, there is a compelling rationale to use the three life-cycle variables illustrated below in Figure 6.3 to generate the model's NCR stream. Users can then study life-cycle track records (the past) and make judgments about likely future track records. The same language is used to understand and communicate about the past and the future. With such a common language in place, users can more easily explain and discuss with others why they are using a particular set of optimistic/most likely/pessimistic forecasts. Different opinions can be debated in a useful way. Experience suggests that the more experience users gain with analyses of historical life-cycle track records, the better their skill will be in forecasting firms' future life cycles.

Figure 6.3: Life-cycle variables that drive net cash receipts (NCRs)

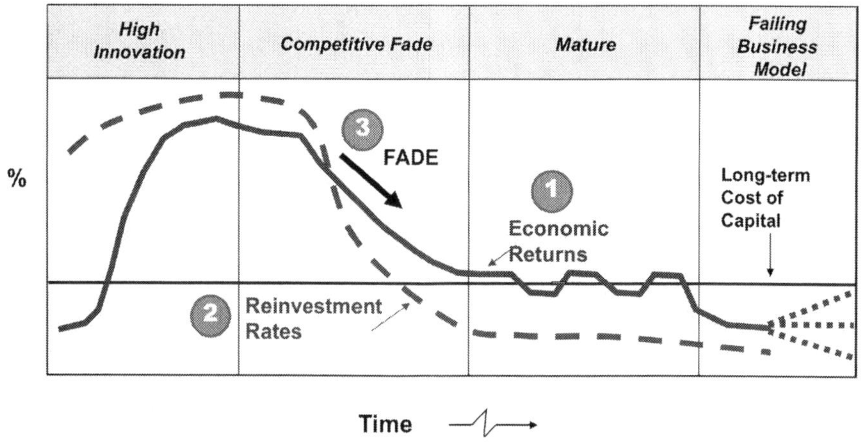

Users of the life-cycle valuation model, seen in Figure 6.4, begin with a calculation of a firm's asset base. The three forecast life-cycle variables drive the calculations for each forecasted year's cash flow, reinvested amounts, NCR, and ending asset base. The firm's *warranted valuation* is then directly calculated. *This is the value warranted by the forecasted life-cycle variables and the discount rate used.* The future NCR stream can be deconstructed into two parts: NCRs from existing assets and those from future investments. The investors' discount rate used will differ from the long-term 6 percent real benchmark shown in the life-cycle figures. Interest rates vary and so do investor discount rates, which is one of the technical topics covered in Chapter 7.

Let's digress for a moment and explain the use of a warranted value instead of *intrinsic value*, which is a much more popular term to use. One needs to be careful about language because giving a name promotes a belief that the thing named exists independently from those using the word. So, after one calculates an intrinsic value, then a stock price above/below this value implies over/under valuation. As such, the stock price is expected to move toward the intrinsic value—like a magnet attracts metal parts. Really? A more plausible orientation is to promote awareness of multiple scenarios (different life-cycle forecasts). The warranted value implies that it is warranted *contingent on* the forecast variables used.

The use of warranted value is consistent with the life-cycle approach that is focused on: learning from historical data, making forecasts, calculating values warranted by the forecasts, and communicating effectively with others. That is truly the *valuation learning process* at work. In contrast to these benefits, pick up any corporate finance textbook and you will read about mathematical present value calculation details and required inputs—but not much about the valuation learning process. Furthermore, textbooks describe economic profit (sometimes referred to as residual income or economic value added) as reported income less a capital charge. Economic profit is an important concept because it puts the spotlight on

the opportunity cost of capital. But economic-profit-based valuation models and their related track records *compress* all the life-cycle variables into
a single number. One problem with this is that it involves the assignment
of a cost of capital that is invariably based on a mainstream finance routine (see Chapter 7), which is notorious for yielding a *wide range of plausible
answers* that radically affect the computation of economic profit. And this
variability remains hidden in the background. In contrast, the decided
advantage of the life-cycle valuation approach used throughout this book
is the "full disclosure" visual display of all the life-cycle components.

Figure 6.4: Life-cycle valuation model

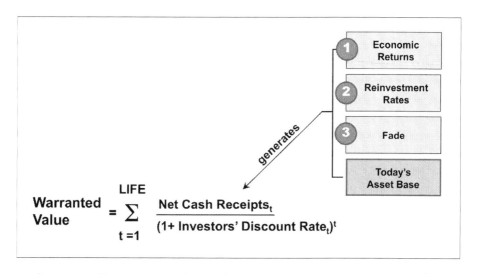

What really causes big, long-term moves in stock prices?

This chapter began with an empirical question as to what really caused
Walmart's 13-fold outperformance of the S&P 500 Index over the 1980 to
1990 time frame. Let's first understand Walmart's position in its life cycle
in 1980. Figure 6.5 shows Walmart at the high innovation stage of its life
cycle in 1980.

Figure 6.5: Walmart life-cycle track record

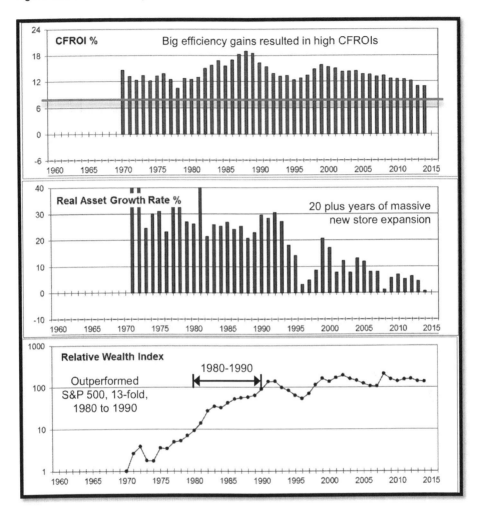

Source: Credit Suisse HOLT global database

To understand cause and effect concerning significant excess (positive/negative) shareholder returns, begin by calibrating market expectations at the beginning of the selected time period; e.g., year-end 1979. Then compare that to the actual life-cycle performance during the period

(1980 to 1990). If a firm delivers performance significantly greater than the market expected, its shareholders almost always will have earned excess returns. Figure 6.6 shows dashed lines as the expected future fade of CFROIs and real asset growth rates built into Walmart's year-end 1979 stock price. With a known market value for Walmart and an estimated investors' discount rate at year-end 1979, the implied future life-cycle fades were calculated using the life-cycle valuation model. In a sense, we use the valuation model in reverse. Instead of calculating a warranted value based on forecasted fade rates for CFROIs and asset growth, we derive implied future fade rates shown as dashed lines in Figure 6.6.

The dark vertical bars in Figure 6.6 represent the actual CFROIs and asset growth rates that were achieved. Now we can see and deal with insightful cause-and-effect relationships. First, Walmart's CFROIs did not fade downward as expected for a typical firm due to competitors duplicating its business model. Walmart's CFROIs actually faded upward as management continued to innovate at a rapid pace. Second, recall the big impact to be had on value due to new investments that earn high CFROIs. All else equal, the higher the real asset growth rate, coupled with above-cost-of-capital CFROIs, the more value is created. Sustained 20 percent-plus asset growth rates during the 1980s, which greatly exceeded year-end 1979 market expectations, were critically important in causing the massive revaluation of Walmart during the 1980s.

With this type of analysis applied to a wide variety of other firms, users of the life-cycle model will gain a deeper understanding of the stock market and purge any remnants of the popular misconception that the stock market is a mystery dependent on the unpredictable emotions of the crowd. The life-cycle valuation model is uniquely useful to investors seeking excess returns as well as to corporate managements and boards that need a valuation compass to guide decision making.

Figure 6.6: Walmart market expectations, year-end 1979

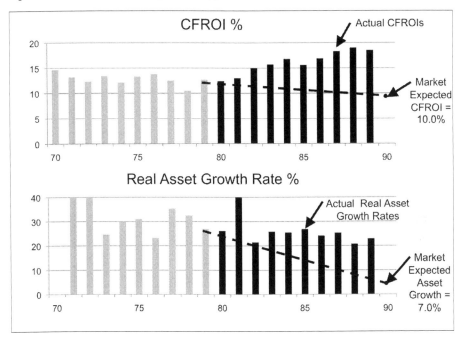

Source: Credit Suisse HOLT global database

The firm's black box, intangible assets, and organizational capital

Ask investors why certain firms achieve wealth-creating economic returns, are able to reinvest significant capital at favorable returns, and achieve favorable fade rates for life-cycle variables. The answers will invariably contain the results of a firm's black box. That is, the firm achieved a commanding share in product markets, high customer loyalty, and the like. But what, really, is causing this outperformance? What is inside the black box?

Competitive advantage rarely comes from tangible assets since these assets can easily be acquired by competitors. Competitive advantage tends to be associated with unique, hard-to-duplicate intangible assets. But many intangible assets (e.g., highly skilled R&D employees) can be duplicated by competitors. The name *organizational capital* is gaining acceptance to represent both the formal and informal processes that determine how shallow or deep the firm's competitive moat is, i.e., the significant roadblocks to attempts by competitors to duplicate the firm's efficiency at delivering value to its customers.

To map out the details of organizational capital is to provide a blueprint for how management can orchestrate a knowledge-building culture that coordinates and seeks to optimize both the tangible and intangible assets that constitute the firm's overall system. The Center for Global Enterprise has embarked on a major research program to better understand the link between organizational capital and competitive advantage. Their report, "Organizational Capital: A CEO's Guide to Measuring and Managing Enterprise Intangibles," notes the following:

> Why do some companies systematically outperform their competitors and maintain their leadership position for long periods of time—some over multiple decades—despite persistent competition and changing business landscape? The answer is organizational capital—a critical part of an enterprise, which every executive should understand how to effectively measure and manage. Organizational capital enables tangible and intangible resources, such as machines, patents, brands, and human capital to be productive. Organizational capital provides the basis for inert resources such as plant and equipment to be combined with intangible assets such as patents, brands and information technology (IT) systems and make them collectively productive.[78]

Keep in mind that "organizational capital" is a provisional name for a complex phenomenon that is not at all well understood at this time.

As our knowledge base increases, our language moves away from broad and vague descriptions and gains in specificity and usefulness. And this surely applies to intangible assets. Consider the term "human capital" or the often-repeated phrase in CEO shareholder letters, "Employees are our most important asset." These are vague terms reflective of limited knowledge. An initial beachhead in this area can be seen in the term "pivotal employees." Research has shown that the retention rate for pivotal employees—typically measured by their past pay progression—is a predictor of firms' future changes in CFROIs. This is a step forward in quantifying the impact of retaining or losing highly skilled employees.[79]

So, what are some of the key components of organizational capital for specific firms? For decades, automotive executives toured Toyota's manufacturing plants, yet did not grasp the role of kata until recently (discussed in Chapter 4). This highly effective, problem-solving mentoring of employees was deeply embedded in Toyota's culture and guided continuous improvement of manufacturing processes—the essence of organizational capital that yields competitive advantage.

One aspect of organizational capital at the Cleveland Clinic is the physical proximity of care givers to patients as part of using medical specialty institutes. The physical gathering of people and equipment in central places, focused on treating particular medical conditions, results in improved patient care. It also accelerates innovation that emanates from physicians from different disciplines interacting in close proximity. This is an excellent example of managerial skill in coordinating both tangible and intangible assets.

If analysts only had access to Koch Industries' historical financial statements, would they *understand* why the firm has generated superior, long-term performance? No. Because they would be clueless about Koch's organizational capital. The key component of Koch Industries' organizational capital is Market-Based Management, which was reviewed in Chapter 5. If MBM is so critical to Koch's performance, why did Charles

Koch explain Market-Based Management in detail in his book *Good Profit?* Why has Toyota been so open in allowing competitors to study their Toyota Production System? Because it is the right thing to do. Fundamental improvements in how people work should be shared for the common good. Moreover, management at Toyota and Koch Industries realize that their relentless emphasis on continual improvement will make it difficult for competitors to match a bar that it is always rising. On a broader societal level, the more we learn about organizational capital, the better equipped managements are to help make employees more productive. This will result in a society's resources being better utilized as well as a higher standard of living.

To sum up the organizational capital discussion, look again at the life-cycle track record for 3M (Figure 2.3). It is very unlikely that 3M had unique physical assets that could not be reproduced by its competitors. Consequently, organizational capital is the key to better understand how 3M adapted and maintained significantly above-cost-of-capital economic returns for the last five and one-half decades. Three hypotheses come to mind concerning 3M's utilizing and keeping their human capital:

- **Esprit de corps**—management's willingness for employees to devote time at work to free-spirited exploration of new ideas likely engendered high team spirit and loyalty. Resigning from 3M to pursue an entrepreneurial startup based on ideas generated while working at 3M would constitute disloyalty.
- **Stickiness**—It may well be that the new ideas generated at 3M tend to involve existing 3M capabilities that would be difficult to reproduce for an employee who might consider leaving to pursue a startup venture.
- **Trust**—3M's adaptability over the long haul in developing new capabilities and extending existing capabilities most likely was done, with rare exceptions, in a way that employees did not fear losing their jobs due to change.

These hypotheses are related to a successful knowledge-building culture.

The need for Life-Cycle Reviews

Have you not experienced that organizations that perform well also communicate well? Whether it be a naval aircraft carrier or a local nonprofit organization, effective communication is a necessary ingredient in order for people to coordinate their work toward achieving a shared goal, routinely identifying problems, and developing and implementing genuine solutions. Managers gain the confidence of their employees when they are able to clearly explain what a goal is and why it is important. In addition, employee confidence increases when managers describe the logic of how performance will be measured so everyone understands the kind of results being targeted. Employees can then take the initiative without being micromanaged. The more complex the system, the greater the need for effective communication.

A business firm with thousands of employees working worldwide is a very complex system. Of great importance in dealing with this complexity is the challenge to understand, manage, and measure the intangible assets that play such a huge role in determining value creation. And, of course, management's performance in creating value is monitored by the firm's board of directors. Moreover, shareholders elect the board and they are justifiably hungry for information that explains how management intends to create value over the long term. Therefore the board needs to coordinate with management and implement a common valuation language that is best suited to: (1) analyze the impact on the firm's value of major, board-level decisions, especially those that deal with strategy and resource allocation, and (2) communicate to shareholders why they should be confident that major decisions are likely to create long-term value. A strong case can be made that the proposed Life-Cycle Review (LCR), explained below, is the preferred means to meet this need.[80]

Let's be clear that all managements and boards use some type of valuation model to guide decision making, whether they are aware of its limitations or not. The model in use might be earnings per share (EPS) growth and rules of thumb for price/earnings multiples, or economic profit/EVA, or a variation of the life-cycle valuation model. The case against using EPS has frequently and effectively been made by finance academics. EPS deficiencies include: the incentive to boost EPS by cutting back on needed investments; or investing in below-cost-of-capital projects coupled with debt financing that can, at times, boost EPS; and more. To avoid EPS pitfalls and incorporate the key cost of capital benchmark, economic profit/EVA became popular. But, as noted previously, economic profit hides the high impact and highly variable cost of capital assignment. And, it does not explicitly reveal the role of reinvestment rates over time. For example, did economic profit rise because of a sale of underperforming assets (negative asset growth) or did it rise due to the much-harder-to-do reinvestment (higher asset growth) in high-return projects (new opportunities) while maintaining a business unit's high economic returns? Would you not want to know?

Decades of practical experience by portfolio managers and security analysts attest to the advantages from the use of the life-cycle valuation model to:

- Gain insights from analyzing firms' and their business units' track records
- Identify key valuation issues and then focus on the likely valuation impacts of alternative levels of reinvestment
- Make judgments, based on experience in analyzing firms' track records, about pessimistic/most likely/optimistic scenarios for future business results

The above advantages are precisely what management and the board need in order to make better corporate decisions as well as document the rationale for those decisions to shareholders.

Life-Cycle Review (LCR) objectives

An LCR has three objectives and is similar in spirit to the board-directed, strategic audit that was proposed by the late Professor Gordon Donaldson of the Harvard Business School:

> The mechanism is a formal strategic-review process ... which imposes its own discipline on both the board and management, much as the financial audit does.... An effective strategic-oversight process requires that the board take control not only of the criteria of performance but also of the database in which the criteria are maintained. One of the problems that outside board members often have in evaluating strategic performance is that all the information they receive passes through the filter of a management perspective. In addition, data often come with limited historical reference and in a format that does not map to the previous one.... The credibility of the board's review process depends on the integrity and consistency of the statistics by which progress is measured.[81]

#1. Value-relevant track records

Display value-relevant track records for the firm and its major business units. Basically, this entails the top two panels of the life-cycle histories shown as figures throughout this and earlier chapters. It requires the estimation of economic returns and the calculation of reinvestment rates for each of the firm's major business units. Management needs to work through the tradeoffs involved with accuracy versus simplicity. Details about the calculation of economic returns, such as the capitalization and amortization of R&D expenditures, need to be explained. The idea is to equip investors with all the information they need. Investors should be enabled to reproduce the economic return calculation or to use alternative procedures if they so choose. Moreover, reinvestment rates need to be broken down to show organic growth as well as the impact of acquisitions and divestitures.

#2 Strategy and reinvestment

Explain both the strategy for value creation for each business unit and the planned expenditures (or divestments) in the context of the unit's past performance (its life-cycle track record). What are the key assumptions that need to be confirmed or disconfirmed for startup businesses? Why should expenditures be committed for nonstartup businesses that have steadfastly failed to earn the cost of capital?

#3 Intangible assets

Provide an overview of how the firm's major intangible assets are utilized to improve business performance. A description of the firm's intangible assets necessarily reflects that the handling of intangibles is a work-in-progress for all firms due to the early stage of our knowledge about this complex issue. This is all the more reason for management to explain their strategy for intangibles along with relevant quantitative metrics. Intangible assets include brand names, reputation, patents, R&D, cultural rules, processes, tacit know-how, employee motivation, and myriad other ways of coordinating work to improve efficiency and promote innovation. They are the keys to value creation for 21st century corporations, and yet we are in the first inning of a very long game to understand how to nurture and eventually optimize their use. Intangibles are viewed as extraordinarily difficult to quantify. Nevertheless, their important impact is reflected in the level of economic returns and reinvestment rates being achieved now, as well as future long-term fade rates for these life-cycle variables. The wrong question to ask is: What is the value of, say, a firm's brand name? In contrast, an effective handling, from the perspective of investors, is to forecast in quantitative terms the impact of the brand name on the life-cycle variables.

Benefits from Life-Cycle Reviews

Here are five significant benefits to firms from implementing Life-Cycle Reviews.

#1 Gain more long-term investors in the firm's shareholder base

Without doubt there is a major benefit from greater transparency and an enhanced understanding on the part of investors about what really drives the corporate results of publicly traded firms. That is, investors gain the confidence to wait for the long-term results of well-managed firms to unfold because they better appreciate what management is working toward. Investors are more likely to be patient with firms not earning the cost of capital if management and the board demonstrate via an LCR that the core problem is recognized and both a strategy and a genuine commitment are in place to deliver much-improved performance in the future. LCRs are the ticket to build up and maintain a base of shareholders who are comfortable in owning the firm's stock for the long haul.

#2 Earn the right to purposively depress quarterly results to create long-term value

Management and boards should stop complaining about "short-termism" and should implement LCRs. That is the answer to the call of many business leaders and academics who have expounded on management's obsession with quarterly EPS that can inextricably shift management into a very bad habit of creative accounting adjustments that eventually are self-defeating. LCRs that display business unit track records, coupled to narratives that explain the business models in operation, set the stage for managements and boards to commit to large-scale investments that may well penalize quarterly operating results in the near future. In a sense, management needs to earn the right to willingly incur shortfalls in quarterly performance and explain to investors why they will benefit from this action. Amazon is a well-known example of such management. Many other firms are capable of following this path if their LCR stories support big investments and give investors reasons to see through upcoming quarterly shortfalls and avoid selling on "weak" quarterly results. Investors want management to invest when their firms are in a strong position to earn well-above-average economic returns. For example, research has shown that when managements of firms in a strong competitive position announce big R&D outlays that will depress near-term quarterly results, their stock prices rise on the news announcements.[82] Managements of business-as-usual firms that steadfastly earn below-cost-of-capital economic returns have little credibility in complaining about the market's impatience with their weak quarterly results.

#3 Improve communications with a common valuation language

Boards of directors need to "up" their game. How many directors actually spend time in board meetings grappling in a meaningful way with the valuation merits of management's proposals? Their primary responsibility is to ensure that management creates long-term value to the benefit of all the firm's stakeholders. To carry out that responsibility effectively, management, the board, and shareholders alike need a common valuation language. Ideally, that language would be based on the life-cycle valuation model and involve LCRs as a working tool.

#4 Apply what is learned from life-cycle valuation principles to executive compensation

It is fair to say that many board members today approve compensation plans for top management without the benefit of applying the well-grounded principles of value creation reflected in life-cycle track records. There is a huge improvement waiting to happen that closely ties management's performance in value creation to their paychecks. LCRs that incorporate the life-cycle valuation model could be the catalyst to make that happen. This would better equip boards of directors to connect compensation plans to long-term value creation and avoid both tying compensation to short-term EPS changes and using stock options that can provide huge payoffs in the absence of above-average management performance. The more directors become engaged with what really drives long-term market values of firms, the more it is likely that management compensation packages will change for the better.

#5 Get engaged with a learning process about intangible assets

Spend an evening studying a firm's 10-K report and tabulate how many numbers really help you understand value creation. You will be disappointed after first being overwhelmed by the mountain of data presented. The problem is that the data are not organized in a way that helps investors understand the past, monitor the near-term, and judge likely long-term firm performance. And the growth of intangible assets makes a bad situation even worse. LCRs are designed to *evolve over time and facilitate learning* among boards, managements, investors, and the accounting rule-makers. A good bet is that the use of Life-Cycle Reviews to communicate about the firm's intangibles is a path forward for managements to get more value from their intangible assets.

In summary, it makes sense for the board and management to first gain experience *internally* with constructing LCRs and using them in their decision-making process. Start with a simple measure of economic return and add complexity only when the benefits of improved accuracy exceed the costs involved. Similarly, start with the capitalization of R&D expenditures as a first step in dealing with intangibles. The eventual goal should be to publish LCRs in the firm's annual reports and use them as part of investor presentations.

The Integrated Reporting movement

Considerable momentum is building worldwide for firms to publish integrated reports explicitly recognizing that shareholders' interests are best served over the long term by taking account of other stakeholders' interests. This movement began with firms being pressured to measure and report the environmental impacts of their business processes. The key organizations involved with integrated reporting are listed below, including highlights from their websites:

- **International Integrated Reporting Council (IIRC)**—"… applies principles and concepts that are focused on bringing greater cohesion and efficiency to the reporting process, and adopting 'integrated thinking' as a way of breaking down internal silos and duplication. It improves the quality of information available to providers of financial capital to enable a more efficient and productive allocation of capital. Its focus on value creation, and the 'capital' used by the business to create value over time, contributes towards a more financially stable global economy.… An integrated report is a concise communication about how an organization's strategy, governance, performance and prospects, in the context of its external environment, lead to the creation of value in the short, medium and long term."
- **Global Reporting Initiative (GRI)**—"We have pioneered sustainability reporting since the late 1990s, transforming it from a niche practice to one now adopted by a growing majority of organizations. GRI's Sustainability Reporting Standards are foundational to this success.… In fact, 93 percent of the world's largest corporations report on their sustainability performance."
- **Sustainability Accounting Standards Board (SASB)**—"The mission of SASB is to develop and disseminate sustainability accounting standards that help public corporations disclose material, decision-useful information to investors.… SASB

is developing accounting standards for approximately 80 industries.... Standards are designed for the disclosure of material sustainability information in mandatory SEC filings, such as a Form 10-K and 20-F."

- **CDP (previously Carbon Disclosure Project)**—"We hold the largest collection globally of self- reported climate change, water and forest-risk data. Through our global system companies, investors and cities are better able to mitigate risk, capitalize on opportunities and make investment decisions that drive action towards a more sustainable world.... In order to protect their long-term investments, institutional investors must act to reduce the long-term risks arising from environmental externalities."

In reading material about the integrated reporting movement you will frequently encounter the words "sustainability" and "value creation." Many times, it is unclear exactly what is meant by those words. "Sustainability" is a term often used to support one's views on how society should be organized. Who could be against sustainability? "Value creation" is also vague when benefits are disconnected from the cost of producing those benefits. And similarly, who could be against value creation?

Sustainability is really about the capacity to endure, similar to how long-lived and adaptable biological systems survive. Hence, sustainable development ensures that organizations, especially business firms, achieve economic progress in a manner that does not make future generations worse off as to societal and environmental concerns. Here is a workable definition of sustainability in the context of a business firm.

A sustainable firm provides employees and customers with an inspiring vision to make the world a better place; efficiently delivers value to its customers, consistent with the firm's vision, thereby earning economic returns, over the long term, that at least equal the cost of capital; builds long-term, win–win relationships with all its stakeholders; and applies creative systems thinking to the design, manufacturing, delivery, and recycling of its products, including their supply chains, so as to reduce waste and harm to the environment.

The above definition directly flows from the four-fold purpose of the firm. Hence, when a firm fulfills its purpose (as described in Chapter 3), it is a sustainable firm.

Integrated reporting promotes systems thinking (integrated thinking), insightful communication, and the development of quantitative metrics for nonfinancial variables that help build win–win relationships with the firm's stakeholders and minimize harm to the environment. These are good things. Proponents of integrated reporting envision mandatory requirements for publicly traded firms worldwide to publish integrated reports. Their vision is that the process of crafting integrated reports will influence management's thinking to the benefit of all the firm's stakeholders. But we should not lose sight of the principal benefit to society from firms—the value customers gain from using the firm's products and services. Robert Eccles, professor of Management Practice at the Harvard Business School, and Michael Krzus, an independent consultant, make the following points in their book *The Integrated Reporting Movement: Meaning, Momentum, Motives, and Materiality*:

> Though less mature than sustainability reporting, integrated reporting is, at its core, a social movement. When put into practice by companies and used by the audience of report consumers, it can transform the way resource allocation decisions are made inside companies and markets across the globe. Its social goal is to use corporate reporting as a means to influence companies and investors such that they incorporate the consequences of the positive and negative externalities of corporate decisions (most typically referred to as "sustainability" regarding social and

environmental issues) and the increasing importance of intangible assets. A key element of this is fostering longer-term thinking and taking more explicit account of all the "capitals" a company uses and transforms in creating value.

... The litmus test for both advocates and skeptics is whether integrated reporting leads to better corporate performance through integrated thinking, all of which should be *ultimately reflected in a company's stock price* [italics added].[83]

On the one hand, care needs to be taken to avoid excessive use of the firm's resources for well-meaning, "do good" activities, particularly when they are unrelated to a firm's business or its skills. Why? Because, from the perspective of society as a whole, the most benefits to the most people occur when resources are efficiently used. This requires a cost-of-capital discipline to be practiced by managements. Investing in below-cost-of-capital projects incurs an opportunity cost, i.e., a foregone project that would have likely created more value.[84]

On the other hand, "shared value" proponents encourage managements to expand their vision for the firm and develop new products and services that are economically sound ways to do good. That is an especially viable way to create value while demonstrating that capitalism is a highly efficient and sustainable means to help those in need. Professor Michael Porter of the Harvard Business School and Mark Kramer, managing director of the nonprofit consulting firm FSG, define shared value as follows:

The concept of shared value can be defined as policies and operating practices that enhance the competitiveness of a company while simultaneously advancing the economic and social conditions in the communities in which it operates. Shared value creation focuses on identifying and expanding the connections between societal and economic progress.

The concept rests on the premise that both economic and social progress must be addressed using value principles. Value is defined as benefits relative to costs, not just benefits alone. Value creation is an idea that has long been recognized in business, where profit is revenues earned from customers minus the costs incurred. However, businesses have rarely approached societal issues from a value perspective but have treated them as peripheral matters. This has obscured the connections between economic and social concerns.

In the social sector, thinking in value terms is even less common. Social organizations and government entities often see success solely in terms of the benefits achieved or the money expended. As governments and NGOs begin to think more in value terms, their interest in collaborating with business will inevitably grow.[85]

In their work, Porter and Kramer distinguish their view of shared value, i.e., what it is and what it is not. Specifically, shared value is about creating both economic value and societal value, and it is not about sharing value already created, which is what philanthropic organizations do. Shared value embraces capitalism as the means to achieve societal benefits, and it is not about one's personal values. Importantly, shared value is a mindset for developing scalable and self-sustaining solutions to society's problems, and this differs from sustainability with its concern for environmental protection.

Let's return to the potential for integrated reports to improve management thinking. Having to explain, in integrated reports, their strategy and the use of the firm's capabilities from an overall systems perspective can be helpful to any firm's management. The adage that clear language and clear thinking go hand-in-hand does have genuine merit. But, many integrated report proponents are striving for a general purpose communication template. This can cause unintended problems. In the case of IIRI's approach, this entails six loosely defined "capitals"—financial, manufactured, intellectual, human, social/relationship, and natural. IIRI argues that an integrated report must address the uses of, and consequences to, all these capitals. This can easily result in diverting management thinking away from the nuts and bolts of delivering value to customers. Instead, management could get drawn into excessive "do-good" activities unrelated to their business skills. *To repeat, the primary benefit that firms bring to society is in efficiently delivering their products and services to customers.*

The concern that management attention can be diverted away from the most essential tasks to deliver value to customers applies equally to how business school students are being taught. Professor Robert Simons of the Harvard Business School notes:

> Business school curriculums have increasingly downplayed the importance of competition in favor of extolling benevolence and virtue. But has the pendulum swung too far? With the constraint of limited attention, has the emphasis on balance, doing-well-by-doing-good, and the quest for enlightenment driven out the focus on competing—the "fire in the belly"—that is the hallmark of winning athletes, winning executives, and winning companies?
>
> ... Many are worried that American businesses are losing their competitive edge. So we should ask ourselves: Are business schools training students to be tough-minded,

winning athletes for the competitive race they will surely face in the years ahead?

Business schools aspire to educate leaders who will make a difference in the world. This means that, first and foremost, business schools should be educating leaders who can create and manage businesses capable of winning in any market. This is the true path for business leaders—and business schools—to make a positive and enduring difference in society and the world.[86]

Winning and competitive advantage involve organizational capital. Previously, organizational capital was noted as a provisional name for a poorly understood process for coordinating and optimizing all of the firm's tangible and intangible assets. Many difficult-to-measure intangible assets surely are part of IIRI's intellectual, human, social/relationship capitals. This brings us back to the point made in Chapter 4 that giving names to the six capitals can yield a false sense that these categories exist independently of those using these words. Giving something a name often is associated with the assumption that one already has reliable knowledge about the thing named. In business, frequently the next step after presuming knowledge about a phenomenon is to promote "best practices." But so-called best practices typically are context dependent, and widespread implementation can lead to all sorts of unintended adverse consequences.

By way of example, recall the previous discussion of Charles Koch's book *Good Profit,* in which he explained in detail how his leadership enabled 100,000 employees to create a $100 billion enterprise by 2014. Instead of using the six capitals, Koch provides exceptionally significant insights *unique to his firm* by using five guideposts: vision, virtue and talents, knowledge processes, decision rights, and incentives. Would Koch's book have been more useful if he replaced his five guideposts with the six capitals? It's hard to believe that.

We have now put a spotlight on a significant problem with integrated reports. Proponents seek codification and standardization to facilitate worldwide regulatory authorities' mandating that publicly traded firms publish integrated reports annually. The problem is that standardization can impede learning, which entails the unique, specific context of individual firms.

Consider again Koch Industries, which has a human resource policy that provides for uncapped compensation for employees. If employees create huge value for the firm, they, in turn, receive a huge paycheck. If this compensation mechanism was assumed to be best practice, independent of context, how might the results be if implemented at the Cleveland Clinic? It would have resulted in unintended, bad consequences since one of the critical cultural changes at the Cleveland Clinic was to put all physicians on a fixed salary in order to achieve much higher overall system efficiency. When dealing with intangible assets, and culture in particular, context matters a great deal.

There is a solution to the standardization/learning dilemma for integrated reports: Life-Cycle Reviews. LCRs have two big advantages that are missing from integrated reports. First, LCRs include the life-cycle track records for the firm's business units, thereby providing a *direct link to valuation*. Second, LCR business unit narratives are meant to read like work-in-process, exploratory reports that are nonstandardized and attuned to unique business circumstances. These narratives would facilitate learning by managements, boards, investors, and accounting rule-makers about how intangibles contribute to value creation. As such, LCRs should be viewed not as competition for integrated reports, but rather as an ongoing means to improve the data and thinking presented in integrated reports. Perhaps, over time, Life-Cycle Reviews would become a part of integrated reports.

CHAPTER 7

The Valuation of Firms Should Be a Continual Learning Process

To break free of the tyranny of short-termism, we must start with those who provide capital. Taken together, pension funds, insurance companies, mutual funds, and sovereign wealth funds hold $65 trillion, or roughly 35 percent of the world's financial assets. If these players focus too much attention on the short term, capitalism as a whole will, too.

… Fund trustees, often advised by investment consultants, assess their money managers' performance relative to benchmark indices and offer only short-term contracts. Those managers' compensation is linked to the amount of assets they manage, which typically rises when short-term performance is strong. Not surprisingly, then, money managers focus on such performance—and pass this emphasis along to the companies in which they invest. And so it goes, on down the line.

—Dominic Barton[87]

Those working in corporate finance, investment banking, or money management have learned the mechanics of using the discounted cash flow method to calculate a warranted value for a firm or business unit. One assembles the forecast inputs, including the selection of a discount rate, and runs an Excel spreadsheet. However, this mechanistic process is less than ideal as a learning experience to improve either forecasting skill or the model itself. *In contrast, the CFROI valuation model and global database are designed to enable users to better understand firms' past performance, pinpoint key valuation issues, decode market expectations, and help judge the plausibility of forecasts.* In addition, the learning process extends to the tough issues of improving the long-term fade forecast and discount rate assigned. This chapter describes the early development of the CFROI valuation model and its related global database, provides an overview about how Credit Suisse HOLT continues this research program today, and presents some ideas that challenge what mainstream finance teaches.

This chapter is for readers who are well versed in finance/valuation and interested in important technical issues. Other readers might want to skip directly to Chapter 8.

Early development of the CFROI life-cycle valuation model

In 1969, Charles G. Callard and I cofounded Callard, Madden & Associates (CMA) and began a research program to better understand levels and changes in stock prices worldwide in order to improve investment decision making. Our initial clients were large money management organizations. Our research program was focused primarily on construction of the life-cycle valuation model (highlighted in Chapter 6), and, importantly, on *processes to continually improve:*

1. Measurement of cash-based economic returns from accounting data
2. Fade forecasts of economic returns and reinvestment rates

3. Estimates of a market-implied (forward-looking) discount rate and the related assignment of investors' discount rates to individual firms

4. Correlations between warranted value calculations and firms' actual historical stock prices for a large universe of publicly-traded firms

In the early years, my focus was on a "model corporation" project (discussed in a later section) that was used to develop the complete life-cycle valuation model, including the translation of accounting data into economic returns, which resulted in the CFROI metric. Callard focused on macroeconomic forecasts and the economic reasons for changes in the market-implied discount rate; i.e., nominal tax rates for interest, dividends, and capital gains, plus inflation. My subsequent 1999 book, *CFROI Valuation: A Total System Approach to Valuing the Firm,* summarized most of this early work. The insights and data about discount rates presented in that book were based on Callard's original discount rate research. The rest of the history about the continued development and later transition of this research program to Credit Suisse HOLT is summarized in the Preface.

Ten critical ideas to connect financial performance to valuation

The following ideas have been an integral part of my long-term valuation research. Many of these ideas evolved from the early CMA work. They are critical in the sense that they guide continual improvement in the four processes noted previously.

#1 Adjustment for inflation/deflation

Key life-cycle variables should be adjusted for changes in the purchasing power of the monetary unit and therefore expressed as *real* variables. This is essential for the analysis of long-term time series so that levels and trends have meaning and are not distorted by inflation/deflation—especially important for trends in economic returns (e.g., CFROIs) and discount rates.[88]

#2 Project economic return

A *project economic return* is the real, achieved return-on-investment (ROI) for a completed project. This internal rate of return is calculated after converting all after-tax cash outflows and inflows into units of constant purchasing power. (In the U.S., this would be done with the GDP Deflator series.)

#3 Cross-sectional economic return

A *cross-sectional economic return* is calculated from balance sheet and income statements for a given year and is consistent with the concept of a real ROI. A RONA (return-on-net-assets) and a CFROI (cash-flow-return-on-investment) are cross-sectional economic returns.[89] Think of the firm as an ongoing portfolio of projects whose conventional accounting statements capture a cross-section of the status of these projects at a single point in time. A plot of the time series of cross-sectional economic returns is used to infer the level of average project economic returns being achieved by the firm. Throughout this book "economic returns" have meant cross-sectional economic returns.

#4 Definition of net cash receipts

With the acceptance of accrual accounting principles, a firm's *net cash receipts* can be calculated in either of two equivalent ways. Figure 7.1 displays how the NCR from the perspective of a firm's operations is identical to the NCR from the perspective of a firm's capital owners. NCRs have a precise definition and do not suffer from the myriad definitions encountered with "free cash flow."

Figure 7.1: Firm's NCR equals capital owners' NCR

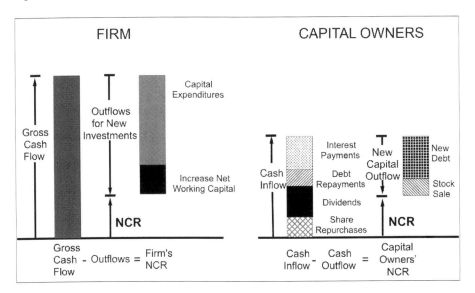

#5 Systems thinking

From a logical perspective, there is a compelling rationale to apply systems thinking to a valuation model. With the life-cycle model, shown in more detail in Figure 7.2, the forecast of future NCRs is highly sensitive to the procedures used to assign fade rates for economic returns and reinvestment rates. Consequently, the assignment of the investors' discount rate should be contingent on how fade rates are forecasted. In other words, the valuation model is a package deal—a total system in which the handling of one component affects other components in the system. Both the early CMA work and HOLT's current global database use investors' discount rates that are based on a market-implied process (discussed below) that is in tune with the fade forecasting routine used.

Investors' discount rates have considerable variability over time due to both changing real tax rates on dividends, interest, and capital gains as well as monetary policy. Since the 2008/2009 recession, quantitative easing by the Federal Reserve has substantially lowered interest rates in the U.S. This plays out in a lower demanded return by a firm's capital owners. With unchanging expectations of future NCRs for the corporate sector, this automatically translates into rising stock prices. Over the last five decades, the investors' discount rate for the aggregate corporate sector has varied above and below the 6 percent real benchmark cost of capital seen in the firms' life-cycle, track-record figures.

But mainstream finance does not use the systems approach. Systems-based logical consistency is ignored by mainstream finance valuation models that parachute a CAPM (Capital Asset Pricing Model)-Beta-derived discount rate into any and all valuation models, ignoring how the users of these models forecast fade rates. A section below deals with CAPM-Beta.

Figure 7.2: Components of the life-cycle valuation model

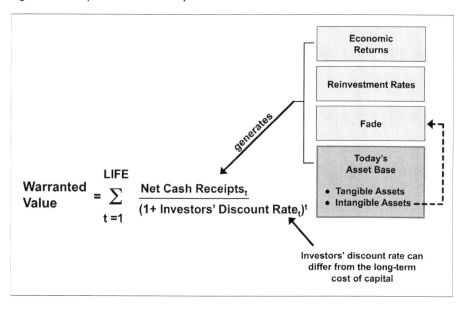

#6 Forward-looking investors' discount rate

How might you assign a discount rate in order to estimate the warranted value of a new municipal bond offering that has not yet been issued? The expected NCRs are already known in terms of interest and principal payments over the life of the bond. With an assigned discount rate, you can calculate a warranted value, which is the expected market price for the bond when it starts trading.

A reasonable approach is to first analyze a large universe of traded municipal bonds and observe the yield-to-maturity and the credit quality of the sponsoring entities. Based on the current market prices for these bonds, you could then plot yield-to-maturity (i.e., the market-implied discount rate) versus credit quality. Then run a regression equation with yield-to-maturity as the dependent variable and credit quality as the independent variable. The resulting regression line provides an *estimated discount rate for a specified level of credit quality*. You would see a higher discount rate for lower quality and vice versa.

The same logic applies to estimating investor discount rates for individual firms.[90] Keep in mind that CFROIs use after-tax cash flows that include the benefit of interest payments being tax deductible. Given this choice, all else equal, higher financial leverage for industrial firms (similar to higher risk for municipal bonds) would motivate investors to demand a higher expected return (higher discount rate). A similar regression approach is used to provide a regression line that ties a market-implied discount rate to a specified level of financial leverage. Other adjustment variables such as trading liquidity can be incorporated via a regression equation. Note that when a firm's stock has less liquidity (wider bid-ask spread and less trading volume), the transaction costs to buy and sell the stock are higher. Consequently, investors should demand a higher expected return to compensate them for the higher transactions costs they incur with less liquid firms. The investors' discount rate for a specific firm is then calculated by inputting the values for the dependent variables used in the regression equation.

The above process requires that each firm in the universe has a fore-casted NCR stream. This is not as easy as the municipal bond example in which forecasted NCR streams were known. The life-cycle model used for HOLT's global database contains monitored NCR forecasts incorporating fade rates that are attuned to near-term consensus analyst forecasts and documented empirical findings about long-term fade rates based on firm characteristics. For example, firms with CFROIs well above the cost of capital tend to fade downward. All else equal, these wealth-creating firms with less CFROI variability will tend to fade downward more slowly. And, all else equal, the higher the reinvestment rate for high CFROI firms, the faster the fade downward due to competitors being attracted to big market opportunities. Firms earning CFROIs approximately at the cost of capital tend to remain there, hence, zero fade. Below-cost-of-capital firms tend to fade up due to pressure to improve operations and/or shrink the business.[91]

The empirical relationships discussed in the paragraph above can be objectively applied to a large universe of firms. All firms that fall within a certain fade-characteristic class are assigned the same fade rate for both their economic returns and reinvestment rates. Although individual firms can have unique company-specific reasons that justify a faster or slower fade than the fade assigned to the class, on average, the fade rates assigned should reflect plausible investor expectations based on a continuation of the competitive process that produced fade rates historically. To sum up, calculated investors' discount rates for firms are contingent on the fade forecasts driving future NCR streams. The closer the fade rate assignments mirror actual fade rates used by investors, the closer will be the estimated discount rates to the "true" discount rates used by investors.

#7 Evaluating the valuation model

From the early CMA work to today's HOLT model, a particularly useful guidepost has been the *value chart*. It plots annual warranted values along-side actual historical stock prices for a firm. The value chart shows how closely the current "state of the art" model (including fade forecasting routines) works to replicate historical prices for firms. Value charts covering a large universe of firms provide insightful feedback about the accuracy of the model and ideas for researching potential "fixes" to improve accuracy.

For any historical year, individual firms have a fade rate assigned based on firm characteristics measured using data available for that year. Actual stock prices can reflect more or less favorable fade rates that were used by investors rather than those used by the model. Also, investors may be using near-term forecasted earnings higher or lower than the consensus analyst forecast earnings used by the model.

Firms with systematic and repetitive, year-after-year over- or under-tracking of warranted values versus actual stock prices is where research attention should be given. Here is an easy-to-follow example. Suppose your valuation model assigned an economic life to a firm's plant and equipment by dividing gross plant by as-reported depreciation charges. If a firm had used accelerated depreciation, the reported depreciation charge would be much higher than economic depreciation causing too low an implied life to plant and equipment. In calculating the present value of cash flows as existing assets wind down over the life of plant and equipment, an abbreviated life would understate the value of existing assets. Consequently, in this situation, warranted values would be expected to track well below actual stock prices. Further suppose that you identify the use of accelerated depreciation and, on logical grounds, decide that an override to straight-line depreciation is appropriate, and this substantially improves tracking on the firm's value chart. Although economic logic is on your side, there is one more piece of evidence to cement the case that this fix is a definite improvement to the model. If you applied this fix to all the firms in your universe that use accelerated depreciation and the entire class of companies greatly improved tracking, then you are on solid ground that the fix should be implemented.

One more example, a bit less obvious, will illustrate the power of this approach in evaluating the valuation model. Note how fixes to your valuation model are similar to the knowledge-building process described in Chapter 4. If your worldview is attuned to systems thinking, you will perceive problems—low correlations between warranted and actual stock prices—as opportunities to orchestrate hypothesis testing and feedback that yields solutions. Every time a genuine improvement is made to your model, the model becomes more robust and able to uncover deeper and more complex problems.

Consider this problem encountered in 2006 for the HOLT model. The regression equation for market-implied discount rates for Taiwanese industrial firms assigned higher discount rates to firms with lower financial leverage. This made no economic sense. Value charts for Taiwanese firms showed, unsurprisingly, low correlations between warranted and actual stock prices. What causes "too high" a discount rate to be calculated? Well, market values are known, so that is not the source of the problem. There must be an error that causes forecasted NCRs to be "too high" and consequently a high discount rate is required to lower the present value to match current market values. Research revealed that CFROIs were excessively high for those companies that were especially generous in dispensing shares for employee stock bonuses. At that time, the Taiwanese accounting rules for net income ignored this true economic expense, resulting in calculated CFROIs being too high. After incorporating an appropriate charge for employee stock bonuses, the problem of higher discount rates for lower leverage firms was resolved. Interestingly, the biggest users of employee stock bonuses were technology companies that had low financial leverage. After a fix was implemented, this class of companies showed significantly improved tracking on their value charts.[92]

#8 Avoid using a CAPM-Beta equity cost of capital

There are three critical questions to ask about any proposed method to assign an investors' discount rate for purposes of valuation calculations. Specifically, does the proposed method:

1. Lead to more accurate valuations than other methods?
2. Advance a process to improve the overall valuation model itself?
3. Help users to better understand how the economic world works?

As to the first question, according to the mathematically elegant CAPM theory, which has extraordinarily deep roots in mainstream finance, a firm's equity cost of capital equals the risk-free rate plus the product of a stock's Beta multiplied by the risk premium of the overall equity market. That risk premium is the expected return of the equity market over the risk-free rate. But, application of the CAPM equation requires two inputs that are extraordinarily difficult to nail down with any precision—Beta and the risk premium. In principle, these are both forward-looking variables; but, in practice, they are estimated from backward-looking historical data. Huge variations in the calculated equity cost of capital can result from plausible but sharply different values for these two variables. This translates into huge variations in calculated warranted values. Even though academic research has made improvements to the standard CAPM-Beta procedure, this standard procedure still holds considerable sway in corporate finance textbooks. A particularly strong argument against use of CAPM-Beta is presented throughout the fifth edition of *Valuation and Common Sense* by Professor Pablo Fernandez at IESE Business School, University of Navarra. See especially his chapters titled "Beta = 1 Does a Better Job than Calculated Betas" and "CAPM: An Absurd Model."

Furthermore, regarding the need for accuracy, keep in mind the earlier point that the parachuting of a CAPM-Beta discount rate into a valuation model gives no regard for how NCRs are forecasted by users of the model. This is not the case with the market-implied discount rate approach integral to the life-cycle model.

In answer to the second question, proponents of CAPM-Beta are silent about how their discount rate approach can advance a process to improve the model itself. Again, this is not the case with the life-cycle, market-implied discount rate approach, as illustrated by the Taiwanese employee stock bonus example.

In response to the third question, in practice users of CAPM-Beta are hard pressed to argue why a certain length of time is "right" for measurement of the risk premium, or similarly for Beta measurement. Fundamentally, CAPM-Beta is a backward-looking process that should be forward-looking and sensitive to change taking place in the current environment. By contrast, the life-cycle, market-implied discount rate approach is forward looking and sensitive to changing market prices. For example, research has shown that taxable equity investors increase their demanded returns to compensate for increased real tax rates due to higher nominal tax rates for dividends and capital gains coupled to the impact of inflation. This makes economic sense and enables changes in real tax rates to be quantified to estimate the impact on investors' discount rates and its related impact on market prices. But this type of research is ill-suited to a CAPM-Beta orientation. To emphasize the usefulness of a market-implied discount rate approach that *does not entail estimates using historical data*, let's consider the following thought experiment.

The logic of the following thought experiment applies to stocks, although, for simplicity, the focus is on bonds. You are asked to forecast the price impact of a surprise news announcement expected next week that instead of interest payments from municipal bonds being tax free, interest payments will be fully taxable. Let's analyze what should happen to the prices of municipal bonds. High net worth investors buy municipal bonds, therefore the maximum tax rate on personal income is the relevant tax rate to apply to investors in municipal bonds. For a specified credit quality, the yield-to-maturity (market-implied discount rate) for municipal bonds is known. This is the return demanded by investors when there is a zero tax rate on interest payments. The pre-tax yield-to-maturity will *increase* next week to offset the new taxes on interest payments. Consequently, market prices for municipal bonds will have to *decrease* to a level low enough to provide the higher demanded return; i.e., the prior week's yield-to-maturity *plus* an additional yield to cover tax payments. The additional yield can be calculated based on the current maximum tax rate for personal income. In summary, this simple thought experiment illustrates how asset prices can change even though their expected NCRs remain constant due to an increase in the investors' discount rate—an increase due to a changed assumption about future tax rates. A similar line of thinking works well to gauge demanded returns by taxable equity investors based on changes in real tax rates for dividends and capital gains.

#9 Intangibles and the art of life-cycle fade forecasting

Capitalizing and amortizing intangible assets is necessary if such treatment materially improves the insights contained in life-cycle track records. R&D outlays have long been capitalized and amortized in the HOLT database because this is necessary to produce meaningful life-cycle track records for firms with big R&D outlays. For example, the middle panel (real asset growth rates) of the life-cycle track records for biopharmaceutical firms is simply misleading if R&D is not part of the asset base. Nevertheless, the estimated economic life used for R&D must be considered as only a rough approximation; but that approximation is better than ignoring the issue. For those intangible assets in which the estimate of a useful life is pure speculation, it is far better to handle in an alternative way. That is, the more valuable the intangible asset (e.g., brand names, patents, and so on), the more favorable the future fade rate.

Let's briefly review some important points about fade rates that will also explain why this section title stresses the *art* of life-cycle fade forecasting. The following approach to quantifying fade forecasts is based on decades of experience working with a large universe of global firms that began with the CMA research in the 1970s. It reflects reasonable judgments that provide plausible valuation answers. Even so, alternative approaches could be developed and evaluated. Figure 7.3 shows the basic fade window.

Figure 7.3: Long-term, life-cycle fade of economic returns

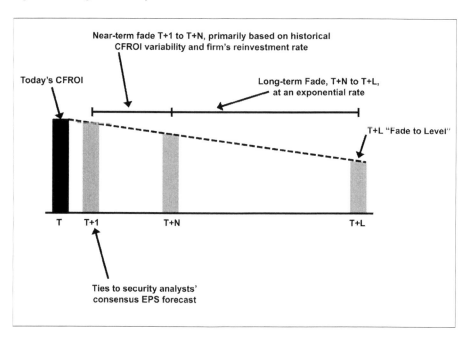

Points related to the figure above follow:
- Long-term fade forecasts are needed for economic returns, reinvestment rates, and today's investors' discount rates.
- An overall fade period of 40 years (L=40) is used with beginning values for economic returns and reinvestment rates set at one year from today (T+1) based on security analysts' forecasts for T+1.
- The long-term "fade to level" for both economic returns and

investors' discount rate is set at 6 percent real. This implies that over the very long haul the corporate sector average return and the cost of capital/discount rate should equalize. The fade-to-level for reinvestment rates is set at 2½ percent real, which approximates the economy's average real growth rate.

- The investors' discount rate transitions from today's level to 6 percent real throughout the 40-year period at a 4 percent per year exponential decay rate.
- Both economic returns and reinvestment rates fade from T+1 to T+N (near term) based on the firm characteristics described earlier. For most firms, a near-term fade window of 4 years is set (N=4). For firms with above-cost-of-capital CFROIs that have demonstrated very low CFROI variability, N can exceed 4.
- Both economic returns and reinvestment rates transition over the long term fade window (T+N to T+L) using an exponential decay rate of 4 percent per year.

#10 A systems-based valuation research methodology

The above points are based on decades of experience with a commercial research program that differs from the way academic research progresses. A key ingredient was feedback from astute portfolio managers and security analysts with detailed country-specific and firm-specific knowledge. They have a vested interest in improvements in the valuation model and its related database that they subscribe to and use for decision making. Their feedback is focused on identifying problems whose solutions can produce practical results in terms of better explaining levels and changes in stock prices worldwide as well as improving forecasts.

Academic research in this area favors mathematically elegant theoretical constructs and advanced statistical techniques geared to publishing journal articles. In contrast, the commercial research program is expansive in terms of firms analyzed and embraces, as noted earlier, continual improvement in measuring economic returns and improving both fade forecasts and investors' discount rates, plus problem solving keyed to deviations between firms' historical warranted values and their actual stock prices. All this is applied to a large universe of firms worldwide that have different accounting standards and different historical inflation environments. Advanced mathematics and statistics—as frequently displayed in the top finance journals—have not been needed.

Figure 7.4 diagrams a knowledge-building loop that encapsulates the commercial research program that began with CMA and continues today at Credit Suisse HOLT. The figure is quite similar to the general purpose loop discussed in Chapter 4. Note that the life-cycle track records, and especially the value charts, *enable problems to be perceived*. Referring to Figure 7.4, accounting fixes most often concern adjustments to more accurately calculate CFROIs. Less frequent fixes involve improved fade forecasts and better estimates of investors' discount rates. Those changes that make economic sense and improve life-cycle track records and value charts are then implemented in the Credit Suisse HOLT database, which now includes over 20,000 firms covering 67 countries. And the knowledge-building cycle continues. Particularly useful is feedback and hypotheses from portfolio managers and security analysts who have deep knowledge about firms in particular countries.

The commercial life-cycle research program, which began with the model corporation (discussed below), was and is heavily focused on the connection between business economics and accounting data. That is a messy, wickedly difficult task not amenable, in my opinion, to elegant mathematical solutions.[93] Here is an example. With a highly mathematical approach, the researcher uses, say, variable "A" for a firm's net assets and proceeds with mathematical formulations while avoiding important practical issues. What about fully retired plant that is still in the gross plant account because it is being used but not included in the net plant account used to calculate net assets? What about R&D that is included as an asset when part of an acquisition, but excluded if internally generated? What about goodwill that is part of acquisition purchase accounting in order to presumably hold management accountable for the full purchase price of the acquisition, but this distorts the measurement of a return on operating assets? What about intangible assets in general? What about assets in countries that experience decidedly different inflation environments? And the list goes on and on. For the most part, labeling assets "A" (or a similar approach using book value as "B") and proceeding with mathematical formulations is the path taken by many authors of academic journal articles that address the measurement of economic returns and the construction of valuation models. What might a different approach look like?

Figure 7.4: The value of valuation tracking problems

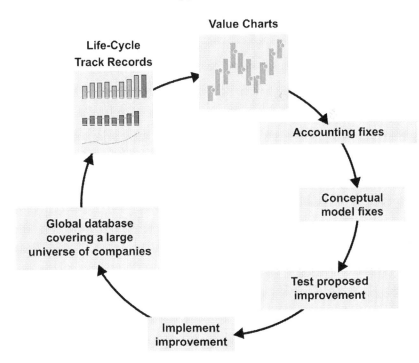

The initial step in order for finance/accounting researchers and their students to gain experience in the methodology practiced in this commercial research program would be to adopt a systems mindset for the *valuation process*. On the one hand, this means treating the components of the valuation model as interdependent. On the other hand, it means that the model itself needs to be constructed in a way that helps users better understand the world so they can make better forecasts. With a systems mindset, the next step is to use an Excel spreadsheet to construct a model corporation that enables known business economics to be translated into conventional balance sheet and income statements that generate an NCR stream so that period-by-period warranted values can be calculated. This model removes the researchers from the comfort of mathematical abstractions and requires them to grapple with a bottom-up approach tied to practical measurement issues. *This provides a tool for experimenting with new ways to use accounting data and information about intangibles to better estimate economic returns.* This approach is well suited for use in learning about the key issues that connect business economics to accounting data and valuation.

Model corporation

Chapter 4, "The Pivotal Role of Worldviews in Building Knowledge," describes the silent but strong pull of worldviews that determine how people perceive problems and devise solutions. One takeaway from that chapter is that an examination of worldviews can help us think about perceptions and gain clarity as to how best to define problems. Let's examine the typical worldview of the accounting rule-makers. They see the need to provide a rule book that provides investors and other users of accounting data with *true earnings*. To accomplish this, revenues must match expenses, and assets are depreciated over their productive lives. So, the rule-makers' perception of the problem is how best to provide true earnings.

This worldview made sense for a world dominated by plant and equipment type assets (tangible assets). But that world where substantial wealth creation was tied to manufacturing scale for chemical, steel, and other manufacturing firms has been replaced by the dominance of intellectual capital (intangible assets). In the New Economy, scale and success are achieved through commercializing ideas, innovative designs, and creative business plans in the biopharmaceutical, Internet, and other intangible-intensive industries. Moreover, those manufacturing firms that are performing well use employees to develop innovative products and services while continually improving core business processes. It is their knowledge-building culture, not their tangible, balance sheet assets, that provides competitive advantage. Tangible assets are easy to acquire and merely owning such assets will not result in achieving above-cost-of-capital returns, whereas a highly productive knowledge-building culture can contribute mightily to superior firm performance.

Would it not be helpful to carefully focus on the key problem investors face in today's world? Let's set aside the assumption that today's investors need true earnings. That assumption automatically leads one to *define the core problem as an accounting problem* when the core problem is actually a *valuation problem*. If there is going to be a stake-in-the-ground, fundamental guidepost that is not true earnings, what is it? The guiding principle should be to provide accounting data and other information that helps investors *forecast firms' long-term net cash receipts*. This needs exists for any and all firms that serious investors choose to analyze.

Handling accounting data and forecasting NCRs is a process that requires a way of thinking—a model—of how the firm operates and how its operational performance is articulated via balance sheets and income statements. This brings us back full circle to the model corporation. That work uses the perspective of the firm as an ongoing portfolio of projects, as illustrated in Figure 7.5. At a selected point in time, the not-yet-completed projects are generating after-tax cash flows reflected on the income statement and their tangible assets still in use are recorded on the balance sheet. A straightforward answer to the value of existing assets at time "T," shown in Figure 7.5, is to calculate a present value for the wind-down (during years T+1, T+2, and T+3) of cash flows from today's projects, including released nondepreciating assets such as land and net working capital.[94]

Figure 7.5: Firm as a portfolio of projects

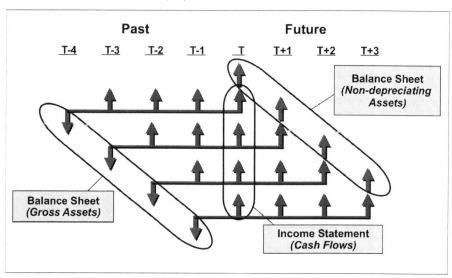

Suppose you were responsible for making an offer to acquire an oil-producing firm. As to the value of existing assets, would you not calculate present values for alternative future NCR streams generated from the wind-down of existing reserves? And the present values would tie into alternative scenarios for future oil prices with related impact on NCRs. That is an eminently sensible approach. Yet, many valuation models, for mathematical convenience, use either book values or today's normalized earnings divided by the discount rate as a proxy for the value of existing assets. Although the mathematical logic of these approaches can be sound, a strong case can be made to focus instead on real world economics. In this example, it means the wind-down of NCRs as existing assets wear out (reserves are depleted).

Returning to Figure 7.5, a complete model of the firm is obtained by specifying a future life-cycle pattern of real project economic returns for each year's investment outlays and reinvestment rates. In this manner, known business economics (projects ROIs and reinvestment rates) generate conventional, period-by-period, balance sheets and income statements. NCRs for each period are calculated, and warranted values of the known future NCRs are also calculated. The model firm operates in an environment using specified inflation rates and interest rates. In constructing an Excel spreadsheet for this life-cycle model, two quality control checks are needed: (1) NCRs calculated from the firm's operations must match the NCRs calculated from the capital owners perspective (see Figure 7.1) and (2) for a zero debt scenario, period-by-period equity shareholder returns (dividends and price appreciation) from owning the firm at prices equal to the calculated warranted valuations must equal the discount rate used in the calculation of warranted valuations.

Working with the model's accounting statements was part of the process to develop the CFROI version of economic returns. In my original model corporation (a Fortran computer program written on punch cards), with proper inflation adjustments, the calculated, cross-sectional CFROIs did, in fact, match the known project real ROIs when these project ROIs were held steady over time. This bottom-up approach for dealing with accounting details may seem decidedly non-elegant versus abstract mathematical models. But this approach is more suitable for generating insights to help with practical performance/valuation challenges.

Let's consider the widely used Earnings/Book metric where Book is the firm's common equity. Figure 7.6 shows the output of a model corporation for a firm with asset composition and financial leverage of a typical industrial firm in the S&P 500 Index. The constructed environment used actual U.S. inflation/deflation rates and interest rates covering a century from 1890 to 1990. For every year, the project ROI was set at 6 percent real. Using the accounting statements produced by the model, the CFROI metric was calculated each period, and it matched the steady 6 percent real project ROIs. How did the "old reliable" Earnings/Book do? Keep in mind that the plant account comprises layers that were affected by widely varying historical changes in the monetary unit—both inflation and deflation—and this, in turn, affects earnings via depreciation charges and book value via the net plant account. The result was a gyrating Earnings/Book over time even though the firm invested every year in projects that repetitively achieved 6 percent real returns. This type of analysis should give pause to mathematical model builders who ignore real-world complexities like the impact of inflation or deflation on historical-cost accounting statements.

Figure 7.6: A century of simulated CFROIs versus Earnings/Common Equity

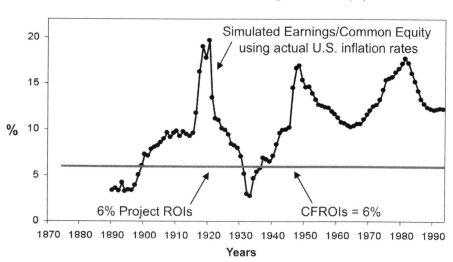

Source: Bartley J. Madden, "The CFROI life cycle," Journal of Investing, Vol. 5, No. 2, 1996, exhibit 4.

Today's HOLT CFROI calculation uses quite a few adjustments to as-reported accounting statements in order to more accurately reflect business economics. Those technical details are addressed in my book *CFROI Valuation: A Total System Approach to Valuing the Firm* and especially in David Holland and Bryant Matthews' forthcoming book *Beyond Earnings*, which includes important technical developments. Shown in Figure 7.7 is the 2014 HOLT calculation of 3M's 15.2 percent CFROI displayed earlier in Figure 2.3.

Figure 7.7: CFROI calculation for 3M, 2014

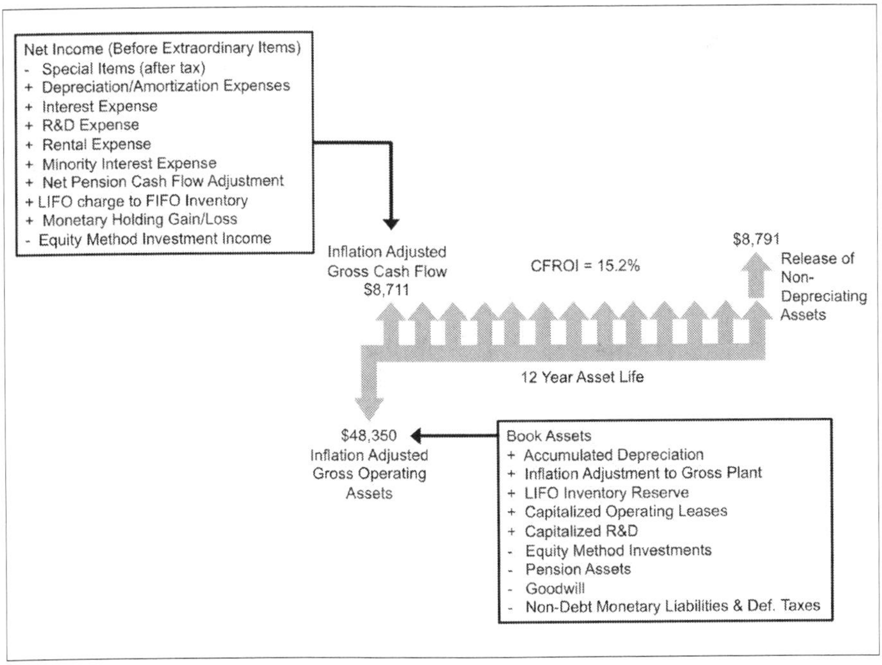

As an aside, I occasionally have been asked why I chose *gross* assets for the CFROI metric as opposed to the *net* assets used in RONA calculations. First, if you begin with a model corporation, then you must deal with project economics that involve initial investment outlays (gross amounts)

and the operating capacity of plant and equipment tied to cash flows. The operating capacity of machines, buildings, and the like does *not* decline as implied by straight line depreciation. And second, the explicit use of economic life forces attention on this variable as to its usefulness for the CFROI computation and for the wind down of NCRs from existing assets. These are important issues that get buried in a RONA calculation. Also, as to existing assets, the wind down of NCRs over the *economic life* of tangible assets for conventional firms doesn't translate so well for asset-light firms. For them, "life" issues need to be analyzed differently, including such issues as the cash burn rate for startups, patent expiration dates, and much more. The one constant is, regardless of asset configuration, firms generate an NCR stream that determines their value.

To sum up, there are tough problems like R&D capitalization, highly specialized project economics, and myriad intangible asset issues that can be productively analyzed using an advanced model corporation. The objective is to gain insights that assist in adjusting conventional accounting data so as to better measure business economics. Management and investors need better tools in order to avoid being fooled by situations such as the false signals of improving/worsening Earnings/Book displayed in Figure 7.6, while economic performance was unchanged.

Future research

A fertile area for research is to develop new approaches for handling economic life issues and calculating economic returns and reinvestment rates that both address a firm's unique intangible assets and facilitate the forecast of a firm's future net cash receipt stream. That research could benefit from incorporating an advanced model corporation capability.

A useful way to begin such a research program would be to define the core problem as improving the accuracy of the forecasted NCR stream. Hence, it is a package deal that involves revised calculations of economic returns and reinvestment rates plus their future fade rates. In other words, instead of attempting to calculate the "true" cross-sectional return that incorporates all the complex aspects of intangible assets, the difficult-to-measure contributions of intangible assets and their longevity would be handled via more or less favorable fade rates. Fade rates are likely to be more intuitive in helping users assess the bottom-line impact of intangible assets.

CHAPTER 8

The Quest for High Performance and Concluding Thoughts

In recent years we have witnessed an endless stream of value-destroying behavior by individuals and organizations in the financial world. The persistence of these scandals—in spite of efforts to curtail them—is, we believe, strong evidence that the prevailing paradigm of financial economics requires transformation.

… [W]e … propose an addition to the generally accepted financial economics paradigm—one that reveals the actual source of these scandals and explains why the best efforts of regulatory agencies and legal authorities have so far failed to stem the tide of value-destroying behavior. We … argue that the core issue at hand is the lack of recognition that integrity (as we define it) is a factor of production that is as important to success in all aspects of life as knowledge, technology and human and physical capital.

—Werner Erhard and Michael Jensen[95]

Erhard and Jensen define integrity as a state of being whole and complete, which is required for maximum workability and a necessary, but not sufficient condition, for achieving high performance. Being whole and complete requires that you keep your word and, in those instances in which you cannot fulfill a promise, you commit to making things right for those who were counting on you. This takes us back to Figure 5.1, which describes one aspect of a high performance culture—ethical standards (including integrity) are nonnegotiable and a code of honor that we practice proudly. Instead of nice-sounding, boilerplate words in a firm's annual report, *ethical behavior* in general, and *integrity* in particular, need to become a lived experience for all employees—which is to say, an integral part of a firm's culture, one that evolves from a firm's fundamental purpose.

The early chapters of this book address the need for clarity about the purpose of the firm and management's core responsibilities. In Chapter 3, the firm's purpose was described as having four interrelated parts: (1) have an inspiring vision, (2) survive and prosper, (3) create win–win relationships, and (4) care for future generations. Clearly, nothing works long term if the firm is unable to survive. To survive, the firm's efficiency in using resources must meet a minimum standard for economic viability, and that standard is to earn the cost of capital. Who has not seen a new business open (restaurant, furniture store, specialty store, and the like) and a few years later the doors are permanently shut? Relative to their competition, their skill in using resources did not warrant continuation of doing what they were doing. However harsh this economic reality is, it serves a needed purpose in continually moving society's resources to their expected best use. This same competitive pressure applies as well to larger business firms, which often can delay needed restructuring due to their scale and access to credit. What we have is the interaction of competition and skill over time and the results that are displayed in firms' life-cycle track records. Every firm can be positioned on a life-cycle chart that displays historical economic returns and reinvestment rates. For publicly traded firms, their shareholder returns versus the general market in the future will be driven by their actual fade rates for economic returns and reinvestment rates as compared to current investor expectations. This is how the business world and the stock market work.

The halo effect

There is a steady demand by those in business and those investing in businesses to learn "proven" ways for firms to outperform competitors. *Be wary of attributing the causes of high performance to characteristics of firms that are judged after their high performance is achieved.* Professor Phil Rosenzweig at the International Institute for Management Development (IMD) in Switzerland labels doing this the "halo effect." That is, ask employees if their firm is a great place to work after the firm has posted a string of highly successful years and most employees will say yes. But this can easily be merely a reflection of high performance and not necessarily a cause of it. Rosenzweig presents a persuasive case that the halo effect led Jim Collins, author of the mega-best-seller book, *Good to Great: Why Some Companies Make the Leap ... And Others Don't*, to make erroneous conclusions.

> Collins claimed to explain why some companies made the leap while others didn't, but in fact he did nothing of the kind. *Good to Great* documented what was written and said about companies that had made the leap versus those that had not—which is completely different. At the start of his book, Collins urges his readers to be honest, to "confront the brutal facts." Well, here's a brutal fact we may wish to consider: If you start by selecting companies based on outcome, and then gather data by conducting retrospective interviews and collecting articles from the business press, you're not likely to discover what led some companies to become *Great*.

You'll mainly catch the glow from the Halo Effect.[96]

In *Good to Great,* Collins classifies management as basically foxes or hedgehogs. Foxes pursue many objectives whereas hedgehogs relentlessly focus on a single objective. Collins stresses that the eleven stellar-performance firms showcased in his book were all led by hedgehog-type top management. So, Collins reasons that being a hedgehog is the way to outperform. Rosenzweig disagrees and argues as follows:

> Imagine that a thousand people spend the day betting at the racetrack, and at the end of the day we select the ten bettors with the highest winnings—we'll call them *Great* bettors. When we look closely at these most successful bettors, we're likely to find that all of them placed big bets on long shots—that's how they came out ahead of the other 990. They were Hedgehogs, focusing on a few big things. Very few Foxes will be among the top ten, because Foxes tend to diversify their positions. Yet even if the top ten bettors were all Hedgehogs, it does *not* follow that Hedgehogs, on average, outperformed Foxes, because some Hedgehogs may have done very well but many more may have gone home broke. In fact, overall Foxes probably did better than Hedgehogs—they took more prudent risks and avoided big losses.[97]

Moreover, even if hedgehogs, on average, did do better than foxes for one particular time period in the past, that same relationship may not hold in future environments. For example, in recent years Amazon, behaving like a fox, has placed many bets as part of an experimental mindset that hugely benefitted its stakeholders. A result of the halo effect is that correlations based on hindsight data can all too easily be confused with reliable cause and effect relationships that do hold in different contexts and time periods.

It isn't just the halo effect that can lead to unreliable knowledge. Our worldviews can inadvertently lead us into betting on unreliable assumptions. A critical part of the knowledge-building loop (Figure 4.1) is that your worldview determines: how you initially perceive a problem, how you can disregard data that actually would reveal a relevant problem, and how you develop hypotheses about solutions. In other words, your worldview puts you on automatic pilot, unaware of the many assumptions being used in shaping how the world shows up for you. *If you reconstruct your worldview to become more aware of the perceptual process at work, you will recognize the limitations of your existing assumptions and become more keenly aware of what you don't know. Such a sharpened worldview would lead to constructive skepticism and experimentation as a way of living that is well suited to fast learning and the purging of obsolete assumptions—the essence of value creation thinking.* The history of Edward Jenner's cycling through the knowledge-building loop in developing a cure for smallpox is a classic example of this kind of experimentation and learning. Moreover, the life-cycle histories of firms document how well or poorly management builds and uses knowledge in order to adapt to a changing world.

Experimentation, feedback, and adaptation

In the two examples that follow, the descriptions of how these firms performed over time necessarily exclude many relevant factors so we can focus, in particular, on knowledge building and experimentation. This focus offers a plausible explanation of how the long-term performance of these firms strongly connects to managements' skill, relative to their peers, in building knowledge and adapting to a changing environment. The following examples—and for that matter, all explanations of the causes of firm performance—need to be critiqued in terms of whether or not the halo effect is at work and likely to lead to erroneous conclusions.

Much can be learned from the historical analysis of firms in industries in which the pace of innovation is much slower than the technology being developed for, say, Illumina's gene-sequencing machines. When the pace of innovation is slow, a firm's culture is especially important to combat the business-as-usual complacency that downplays the need for innovation. All firms need to adapt to changing times, the only difference being the speed at which the adaptation needs to take place. A large firm with a rigid bureaucratic culture in which employees feel that a paycheck is earned just by showing up for work, not what they accomplish at work, is a recipe for eventual bankruptcy and significant loss of jobs and shareholder value. The example that follows illustrates that the required pace of adaptability can well be slower in certain industries, but that does not eliminate the need for effective experimentation and learning.

JCPenney's life-cycle transition

James Cash Penney was 26 years old when he opened his first retail store in 1902 in Kemmerer, Wyoming, a coal mining town. He was a forerunner of Sam Walton in his extreme focus on providing the best goods at the lowest price. He became legendary for his attention to detail in order to improve efficiency. For example, he demanded that every piece of string and every piece of paper that entered his stores be reused. He understood deeply the value of win–win relationships. In the early years, he gave equity in his stores to the hard-working store managers who embraced his principles.[98] His principles were:

- To serve the public, as nearly as we can, to its complete satisfaction.
- To offer the best possible dollar's worth of quality and value.
- To strive constantly for a high level of intelligent and helpful service.
- To charge a fair profit for what we offer—and not all the traffic will bear.

- To apply this test to everything we do, "Does it square with what is right and just?"

The above principles, crafted in the early 1900s, were practiced by the boss, and so the stage was set for all employees to follow in his footsteps. His principles provided the firm with an extraordinarily sound foundation to build on. By 1950, JCPenney was the largest retail department store in the world. Over the years, management experimented with different types of merchandise, including hardware, appliance, and automotive departments, all of which were later discontinued; purchased a bank in order to issue its own credit cards; built up and then sold a direct-marketing insurance business; acquired drug store chains that were later divested; and more recently, developed an Internet business. To sum up, JCPenney's core business benefitted from its large scale and was a steady performer, while its forays into new areas never duplicated the success of its core retail store business. The firm's life-cycle track record covering 1960 to 2014 is shown in Figure 8.1.

In this figure, the firm's CFROIs were almost always at, or for most years well above, the benchmark 6 percent real cost of capital until 2011. Since 2011, JCPenney has encountered particularly serious shortfalls in financial performance. This was due to formidable competition from Walmart, Target, Amazon, and other retailers, and especially due to a failed large-scale overhaul of stores that was implemented by a new CEO.

What type of culture permeated JCPenney at the beginning of its rapid decline? In January 2012, the chief operating officer was quoted in the *Wall Street Journal* as saying he discovered that 30 percent of the Internet usage by corporate headquarters staff was for personal viewing of YouTube videos. Not good.

Figure 8.1: JCPenney

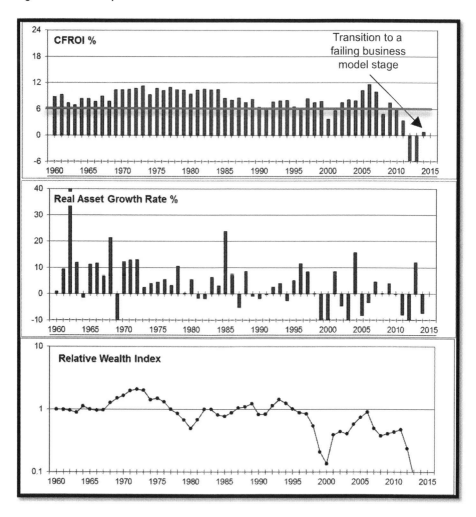

Source: Credit Suisse HOLT global database

Ron Johnson was hired as CEO in November 2011 after being responsible for the hugely successful rollout of retail stores at Apple. He hired many former Apple executives who then worked as a separate tribe and avoided collaboration with other employees. Large layoffs hit and morale

186

plummeted. Worse, Johnson implemented a radical overhaul of JCPenney's stores without any small-scale testing. When a colleague suggested that testing was needed before rolling it out to all the firm's 1,100 stores, Johnson replied, "We didn't test at Apple." You may recall that during Johnson's time at Apple, Steve Jobs was famous for asserting that customers don't know what they want until you give it to them. The subsequent catastrophic decline in sales at JCPenney is a telling reminder that past experiences shape assumptions and context matters. JCPenney's board quickly fired Johnson and then rehired the CEO whom Johnson had replaced.

Intuit's learning culture

Scott Cook and Tom Proulx founded Intuit in 1983 to deliver software to help customers pay bills, maintain their check registers, and review expenditures. The firm's culture originated with Cook's extraordinary concern for customer satisfaction, first-hand customer feedback, and using an *experimental mindset as if you didn't know what customers experience and want*. Intuit's financial software was designed for exceptional ease of use (intuitive), which led to the corporate name Intuit.

Cook's crusade to establish a long-lived "customer evangelist culture" at Intuit was remarkable due to its intensity. It was highly successful. Engineering and marketing employees would accompany first-time customers using the firm's flagship product, Quicken, and observe them install and use the software. In the early years, Cook required every employee to get involved with answering service and support calls, and resolving customer difficulties. This led to a shared bond throughout the firm that focused on eliminating the sources of customer problems so customers would recommend to their friends that they purchase the software that was so easy to use. Furthermore, Cook told his employees:

> No matter what your business problem is, talk to your customers or prospects in depth. Listen intently. Some of the

biggest wins in business are the paradigm shifts that do not come from current wisdom. Those major wins only come from bathing yourself in and swimming with the customer. Reorient your priorities and view of the world to what the customer really wants.[99]

After beating Microsoft's Money, a competing product to Quicken—no small feat for a firm that was only a small fraction of Microsoft's size—Intuit management decided to address the needs of small business owners who could not afford a full-time accountant. The result was QuickBooks, which continued the firm's customary ease-of-use trait. Intuit later acquired TurboTax and, similar to its other products, made this tax preparation software the leader in its category. In the life-cycle track record shown in Figure 8.2, note how CFROIs plummeted after Intuit's 1993 IPO. That was because a 1994 acquisition of Parsons, with its many different types of consumer software, was a poor cultural fit. Also, a raft of new products was developed, but their sales potential proved to be limited. Then a failed merger in 1995 with Microsoft consumed a great deal of management's time.

In 2008, Brad Smith became CEO and led Intuit on an accelerated path of innovation that resulted in CFROIs holding their lofty level and not following the typical fade downward. Prior to his arrival, the core products had been incrementally improved over time, but this did not measure up to his standard of *design for delight* that encompasses customers' emotional experiences with all aspects of Intuit's products. For example, Smith's team developed SnapTax, which enables customers to use their smartphones to take a picture of their W-2 forms and then directly transfer this information to TurboTax for income tax filing preparation. Customers love this app that lets them e-file their federal and state returns from their smartphones.

Figure 8.2: Intuit

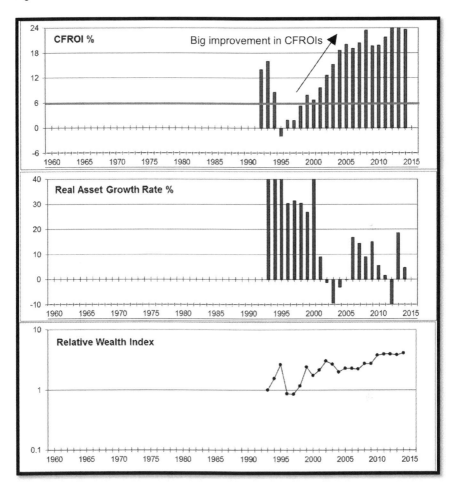

Source: Credit Suisse HOLT global database

On Intuit's website, Brad Smith explains his belief about the most important job of a CEO:

> As a public company CEO, I can safely say this is the one
> aspect of being a CEO that rises above the rest—*creating*

a strong company culture. The culture you create lays the foundation that enables every other part of the company to grow and succeed.... job one in creating a culture is building a *purpose-driven culture.* What is the mission of the company? What is the bigger idea that we are all part of? It is the CEO's job to articulate and communicate this purpose across the company, so team members at every level have something to rally around. At Intuit, our mission is to improve our customers' financial lives so profoundly they can't imagine going back to the old way.

... One way leaders can create an action-oriented environment is to match inspiration with rigor, adopting a rapid experimentation culture. Great ideas are simply hypotheses unless matched with tangible proof they deliver meaningful impact. A rapid experimentation culture cuts through hierarchy (especially if leaders hold their own ideas to the same scrutiny of testing), creating an environment where everyone can innovate, and "debate" turns into "doing."[100]

The viewpoint above succinctly communicates that long-term value creation begins with clarity about the purpose of the firm and management's core responsibilities. It is notable that Brad Smith clearly "gets it" that culture has its roots in management's behavior and that employees are far more likely to buy into a knowledge-building culture when the firm's leaders "hold their own ideas to the same scrutiny of testing." In a very real sense, how employees (especially management) *think* can become a unique competitive advantage.

Strategy and execution

The words "strategy" and "execution," like other names for things, often promote a view of stand-alone independence—the opposite of systems thinking. With this view, strategy is developed and then handed off to those responsible for executing the strategy. This reflects a worldview with significant limitations. A recurrent theme in this book is the use of systems thinking and the value that can be achieved from reconstructing your worldview in order to avoid automatically accepting assumptions—assumptions that are often camouflaged by language. In summary, the four core beliefs that work to improve one's worldview are: (1) our past experiences shape assumptions, (2) language is perception's silent partner, (3) we improve performance by identifying and fixing a system's key constraints, and (4) our behavior is control of perception. Next, let's focus on how language (core belief 2), and especially systems thinking (core belief 3), can help resolve the sharply different opinions frequently heard about the importance of strategy versus execution.

One side of the debate asserts that strategy is vastly more important than execution in achieving competitive advantage because it is more doable to design a strategy that diverges from your competitors. Strategy proponents argue that firms tend to quickly duplicate "best practices" in regard to execution, thereby eliminating any hope of gaining competitive advantage. Proponents of execution reply that strategy is fine, but that skill in getting things done is a hallmark of high performers and that the lack of execution skill haunts those who fall by the wayside.[101]

Figure 8.3 expands on the previously presented Figure 3.3 and emphasizes a systems view. That is, strategy and execution are *connected* to both the firm's knowledge-building culture and its long-term life-cycle performance.

Figure 8.3: Strategy and execution as part of a system

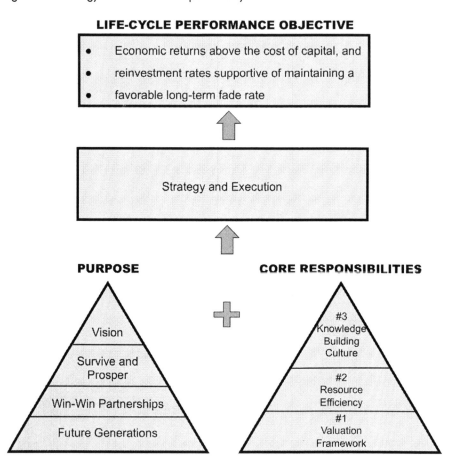

The diagram shown in the figure suggests that a knowledge-building culture is foundational to the process of evolving a strategy as well as the process of continually improving operations (execution). At bedrock, the knowledge-building loop (Figure 4.1) is a way for both management and other employees in the firm to work smarter. The right culture enables everyone to systematically learn, thereby leading to better strategy and better execution. For example, the lean paradigm, epitomized by the Toyota Production System with its focus on kata (Chapter 5) to guide behavior, instills scientific thinking and continual experimentation in order to identify and eliminate waste. This is fundamentally about how work and continual improvement is done—let's label it *execution,* for sure. Getting an entire organization to embrace this way of working is hard to do, and accomplishing this can certainly contribute to competitive advantage. Some lean firms, such as Danaher, extend this kind of competitive advantage even further because they have learned how to acquire firms and quickly get the new employees to embrace their lean culture.

Successful lean firms have business unit managers with a high cognitive skill in finding and eliminating the sources of waste. That skill can be applied, not only to their own firm, but also to their customers' operations. This leads to a bottom-up strategy of developing new products and services that can be demonstrated to eliminate waste and improve performance for customers' business processes. Along these lines, another aspect of execution that contributes to competitive advantage is reflected in highly adaptable organizations that are skilled at fast cycle times (fast execution) in developing new products attuned to customers' high-priority technological needs.

Finally, many believe that strategy is what "really smart" top-level managers do and then hand it off to be implemented. Well, really smart leaders, as illustrated by the Intuit example, are aware of the need to *involve others in systematically experimenting and learning, with particular attention given to customer feedback.* Strategy and execution are part of a continual learning process that is at the heart of a knowledge-building culture that involves all the firm's employees.

A path forward

I hope that, at this point, readers will have gained some useful ideas about value creation. One takeaway they might have is the need for systems thinking that connects things such as how strategy and execution share a connection with a knowledge-building culture. Similarly, business firms do not operate as independent entities in total "control" of their long-term performance. They operate as part of a societal culture that we should want to be supportive of value creation, similar to how a high-performance culture for a firm promotes value creation. We should all want free-market capitalism to triumph over crony capitalism. Others have reached the same conclusion. John Mackey uses the term "conscious capitalism," declaring that "business ... is heroic because it lifts people out of poverty and creates prosperity." Charles Koch, says "good profit comes from ... creating superior value for our customers while consuming fewer resources and always acting lawfully and with integrity." These different words convey the same message: that America needs a level competitive playing field in which value created is shared in approximate proportion to the contribution made, thereby nurturing an opportunity-rich society in which people can rise as high as their skills and determination can take them.

In my opinion, key ingredients have been missing in the current debates about capitalism, inequality, short-termism, executive compensation, corporate allocations of resources, and other major intellectual hot spots concerned with business firms. What is needed, in my view, is an insightful understanding of how business firms create value over the long term and how that value is reflected in stock prices. The thrust of this book, displaying long-term track records of value creation and dissipation, is to promote the life-cycle valuation framework as the sensible way to meet these needs—a way that enables us to better understand history as well as to improve management practices. The pace of adoption of the life-cycle framework in the corporate world depends on people experiencing benefits from using this framework. At the corporate level, the Life-Cycle Reviews proposed in this book would be a giant step forward, as they would yield benefits from experimentation and learning about measuring corporate performance using a long-term perspective as well as from improved resource allocation decisions. Implementation of

Life-Cycle Reviews would also provide a uniquely useful communication tool that benefits investors in general and those with fiduciary responsibility for large pools of capital in particular.

In conclusion, the ideas in this book offer a path forward for managements and boards to deliver enhanced firm performance, driven by employees who trust in management and share a purpose with them. All of a firm's stakeholders would benefit.

Notes

CHAPTER 1: Capitalism and Economic Progress

1   Mackey and Sisodia (2013), p. 21. See the related website, conscious-capitalism.org.

2   From "Created Equal," an episode of the PBS television series *Free to Choose*, 1980, vol. 5 transcript.

3   Thomas Edison did not simply invent the incandescent electric light bulb. He developed a *system* of electric lighting whereby candles and gas-fired illumination became obsolete, Israel (1998).

4   Hernando de Soto makes a compelling case of enormous practical importance that the lack of formal property rights is the source of poverty in poor countries. See Soto (1989) and (2003).

5   Phelps (2013), p. vii.

6   Bessen (2015) argues that politically influential interests have moved government policies away from learning on the job, which is especially important for gaining technical knowledge. He notes on pp. 225–27:

> [T]he institutions that matter are not just those that provide incentives to entrepreneurs and inventors but also those that encourage large numbers of ordinary workers to acquire new skills and

knowledge.

... Yet the policies that inhibit the growth of wages for the median worker today are driven by a broader set of interests than the concerns of the top 0.1 percent. The professional associations that lobby to raise educational requirements for occupational licensing are not composed of billionaires. Nor are most of the shareholders of the defense contractors or electronic health system vendors who fight open standards. Nor are the lawyers who lobby against fixing the patent system. The members of these interest groups are well off, to be sure, but they are not billionaires. The relative wealth of the top 0.1 percent might not matter much to the economic health of the average worker. The obstacles to restoring wage growth might have more to do with the broader dysfunction of our dollar-dominated political system than with the particular role of the extremely wealthy.

Hanushek and Woessmann (2015) present extensive empirical evidence that long-run prosperity is critically dependent on the knowledge capital of a nation. Moreover, they emphasize the importance of *acquired skills*, not time in school, in explaining economic growth. Hence, they argue that, for the educational system, policies should focus on student outcomes, e.g., demonstrated proficiency in math and science.

7   Baumol (2002), Bhidé (2008), McCloskey (2010), and Ridley (2010).

8   Allison (2013) and Allison (2015).

9   Center for Ethics and Entrepreneurship, "Interview with John Allison," July 19, 2011.

10 House Committee on Science, Space, and Technology, Subcommittee on Technology, Environment, and Aviation, "High Technology

Innovation: Free Markets or Government Subsidies? An Entrepreneur Endorses the Invisible Hand," March 25, 1993, Statement of Dr. T. J. Rodgers.

11 Mackey and Sisodia (2013), p. 3.

12 Rajan and Zingales (2003), pp. 275–76.

CHAPTER 2: The Firms' Competitive Life Cycle

13 Stigler (1963), p. 54.

14 Christensen and Kaufman (2008), p. 1.

15 Rose (1928a).

16 Brayer (2006).

17 Larish (2012).

18 Lev (2012), pp. 225–29.

19 Comfort (1962), Gundling (2000).

20 Hindo (2007).

21 Timmerman (2015).

22 Christensen and van Bever (2014), p. 67.

CHAPTER 3: The Firm's Purpose and Management's Core Responsibilities

23 Bower, Leonard, and Paine (2011), pp. 180 and 194. The authors make a strong case that managements and boards should lead the way in securing a market-based, capitalist society in the future. They believe that, instead of seeing themselves as bystanders, business leaders must

engage in strengthening institutions at the community, national, and international levels. Their Chapter 7, "Leading Through Institutional Activism," resonates with the ideas in Colander and Kupers (2014).

24 George (2003), p. 66.

25 An exceptionally innovative course, "Humanomics," is being taught at Chapman University. The three guiding questions for the course are: What makes a rich nation rich? What makes a good person good? And what do these questions have to do with one another?

26 Jensen (2001), pp. 12 and 14.

27 Friedman (1970).

28 Philipson and Jena (2006) and Nordhaus (2004).

29 Bezos (2011).

30 Mackey (2005).

31 Stewart (2013).

32 Womack and Jones (2013), p. 10.

33 Johnson (2007), P. 13.

34 DeLuzio (2001), p. 8.

35 Fuller and Jensen (2002).

36 Graham, Harvey, and Rajgopal (2006), p. 31.

37 Stone (2013), p. 12.

38 Bezos (1997).

39 Bezos (2008).

CHAPTER 4: The Pivotal Role of Worldviews in Building Knowledge

40 Hess (2014), p. 75.

41 This quote is from the Foreword to Brothers (2005).

42 Gregory (2009), p. 10.

43 Frith (2007), pp. 17 and 132.

44 See Madden (1991) and (2012a). In Klein (2013), you can read entertaining and highly educational descriptions of how people form insights in *natural settings*. For an excellent discussion of the differences between Klein's naturalistic decision-making approach and Daniel Kahneman's (2011) focus on heuristics and biases, see Kahneman and Klein (2009).

45 Rodriguez (2006).

46 Bazin (2000), p. 39.

47 Rumelt (2011).

48 Walton (1992), p.140.

49 Zapolski and DiMaggio (2011), pp. 24 and 25, note the following:

> Responsibility—acknowledging our cause in the matter, seeing where we have been inauthentic, taking whatever actions we need to take, and telling the truth about it—is key to restoring and having power.
>
> … Access to restoring our power resides in language.… Our ideals, standards, and expectations occur in language. Our reluctance, accommodation, and powerlessness occur in language. But language is also the home—the only home—of possibility. What determines whether possibility (a creative act) or failed possibility

(an ideal masquerading as possibility) will carry the day is up to each of us. The choice is ours.

50 Broadly speaking, Zaffron and Logan (2009) are concerned with systems thinking and phenomenology, which is inquiry into the nature of lived experience. Along these lines, see Bortoft (2012) for a discussion of "authentic wholeness" and a "dynamic way of seeing," and Robinson and Robinson (2014) for the application of these concepts in business.

51 Eli Goldratt had a unique ability to analyze complex problems and develop exceptionally insightful solutions based on discovering fundamental cause-and-effect relationships. His processes for systems thinking and his focus on identifying and fixing a system's key constraint should be taught to all business students. For a short overview of his way of thinking, see Goldratt and Goldratt-Ashlag (2008) and Madden (2011). Cox and Schleier (2010) is a comprehensive handbook discussing important topics related to Goldratt's theory of constraints. Consistent with the spirit of *Value Creation Thinking*, the following quote is from Goldratt's Introduction to the first edition of his mega-best seller, *The Goal: A Process of Ongoing Improvement*:

> The secret of being a good scientist, I believe, lies not in our brain power. We have enough. We simply need to look at reality and think logically and precisely about what we see. The key ingredient is to have the courage to face inconsistencies between what we see and deduce the way things are done. This challenging of basic assumptions is essential to breakthroughs. Almost everyone who has worked in a plant is at least uneasy about the use of cost accounting efficiencies to control our actions. Yet few have challenged this sacred cow directly. Progress in understanding requires that we challenge basic assumptions about how the

world is and why it is that way. If we can better understand our world and the principles that govern it, I suspect all our lives will be better.

52 Tett (2015) uses an anthropological lens to analyze the degradation in organizational performance due to individuals working in silos of thought, process, and product. Tett's focus on silos resonates with the ideas on worldviews discussed in this chapter. On p. 28 she notes:

[There] is a tendency to use formal and informal classification systems and cultural rules to sort the world into groups and silos. Sometimes we do this in a formal manner, with diagrams and explicit rules. But we often do it amid thousands of tiny, seemingly irrelevant cultural traditions, rules, symbols, and signals that we barely notice because they are so deeply ingrained in our environment and psyche. Indeed, these cultural norms are so woven into the fabric of our daily lives that they make the classification system we use seem so natural and inevitable that we rarely think about it at all.

53 In their article "A century of psychology and psychotherapy: Is an understanding of 'control' the missing link between theory, research, and practice?" Warren Mansell and Timothy Carey (2009) point out:

The ability to view the brain in action forces us to confront some basic truths—we are biological beings—and what we call "beliefs," "attitudes" or even "working memory" do not exist in the same tangible sense as a chair or a duck; they are essentially functions carried out by coordinated networks of cells that form the brain. William James took a functionalist view of the mind, which seems apparent in today's cutting edge science. Interestingly, it is now established that throughout the sensory cortex, the neural pathways sending signals down from higher order areas of the brain, such as the frontal regions, are at least as substantial as those sending signals in the traditional, "input" direction. It seems that at every level of perception, top-down information is utilized, or integrated in some way, with incoming signals from the sensory organs. While this evidence fits with cognitive approaches, it is particularly consistent with a view of the brain as a purposeful organ that guides and regulates incoming perception.

There is a great deal of published material on PCT. Listed below are suggested readings, beginning with the most basic and leading up to more advanced technical material.

(a) A useful beginning point is to visit these websites: pctweb.org, iapct.org, and livingcontrolsystems.com.

(b) Bill Powers (1998) is an easy-to-read PCT overview. Powers (2005) is the classic statement about PCT. Cziko (2000) describes how PCT connects to the work of Claude Bernard and Charles Darwin. Yin (2013) provides an insightful discussion of the role of PCT in restoring purpose in behavior.

(c) Marken (1992), Marken (2002), Runkel (2003), and Forssell (2009). See Powers (2001) for an historical overview of negative feedback control.

(d) Powers (1989), (1992), (2008).

For an application of PCT to sociology see McClelland and Fararo (2006). See Carey (2006) for a method of psychotherapy based on PCT principles.

54 Barrett (2011), pp. 99-100, makes a persuasive case that thinking and behavior constitute a property of the whole organism, not just the brain. Her analysis is supportive of perceptual control theory:

[A]nimals act on their environments, and are not merely acted on by them.... behavior is not the result of a one-way link that goes from stimulus to response, but a loopy process of "sensorimotor coupling" in which action and movement often precede sensory stimulation. This reversal of our usual way of thinking allows us to recognize that, ultimately, behavior is about controlling one's perceptions.

... PCT therefore argues that the reason why behavior varies is that animals are trying to maintain stability in their perceptions of the world. So, like Gibson's and Dewey's theories, PCT is also a theory of behavior that considers animals to be "purposeful": an organism controls its own behavior, and hence its own fate, by its actions in the world. Its purpose is to defend its internal states (i.e., to sustain homeostasis) and the external state of the perceived world, so that it remains within certain limits that are conducive to its survival.

55 Amabile and Kramer (2011), p. 10.

56 Adner (2012), pp. 17–23.

CHAPTER 5: The Firm's Foundational Culture and Business Performance

57 Gerstner (2002), pp. 117 and 189.

58 Schein (2010)

59 Guiso, Sapienza and Zingales (2013).

60 Neffinger and Kohut (2013).

61 The General Electric and General Motors examples were originally used in Eccles and Nohria (1992), pp. 31–34.

62 Senge (2006), p.165.

63 In Womack (2011), pp. 68–71, Jim Womack describes two distribution centers that were quite similar in tangible assets but radically different as to management's respect for employees. One trusted employees to solve problems, and the employees were continually coached to improve standardized work processes. The other facility focused on hitting production targets without any standardized work processes, and employees were not coached in problem solving. The former had twice the productivity as the latter with little turnover of employees, while the latter had to replace 70% of their work force each year.

64 Shook (2010) and Glass (2010).

65 Shook (2010), p. 68.

66 Rother (2010), pp. 101 and 165.

67 Ibid., pp. 139–40.

68 Cosgrove (2014), pp. 12–13.

69 Ibid., p. 25.

70 Merlino (2015), p. 79.

71 Whole Foods website, WholeFoodsMarket.com, Declaration of Interdependence, accessed March 13, 2016.

72 Koch (2015), pp. 4–7.

73 "GM CEO: People died in our cars." September 17, 2015. CNN Money.

CHAPTER 6: Valuation insights, Life-Cycle Reviews, and Integrated Reporting

74 Jensen and Fuller (2003).

75 "Letter from the Founders: An Owners Manual for Google's Shareholders," Google Inc. Form S-1 SEC filing, April 24, 2004, pp. i–vi.

76 Hand and Lev (2003), Corrado, Haltiwanger, and Sichel (2005).

77 In my 1999 book, *CFROI Valuation*, a performance scorecard was presented that showed a firm's % Future, which was based on a stock price as of a specific date. The estimated value of net cash receipts from the wind-down of a firm's existing assets was subtracted from the firm's total market value (equity plus debt) to yield an implied value for future investments. The value for future investments is then expressed as a percentage of the firm's total market value. This calculation is used for the % Future, or Innovation Premium, that plays a prominent role in *Forbes Ranking of the World's Most Innovative Companies*. See my website, ValueCreationThinking.com, for an up-to-date scorecard with % Future for 1,000 U.S. industrial firms.

78 Lev, Radhakrishnan, and Evans (2016), p. 5. See also thecge.net.

79 Ubelhart (2009) used a unique database of Hewitt Associates covering 1,000 firms and 20 million employees. Empirical results include the finding that a significant loss of pivotal employees (defined as top quartile percentage pay progressors, adjusted for age, pay, and tenure) *predicted* future shortfalls in financial performance. See also Frigo and Ubelhart (2015) and (2016).

80 I originally labeled Life-Cycle Reviews as Shareholder Value Reviews and explained this concept in Madden (2007a), (2007b), and (2008).

81 Donaldson (1995).

82 Tong and Zhang (2014).

83 Eccles and Krzus (2015), pp. 59 and 99.

84 Frigo and Litman (2007) offer guidelines to "... assist management in choosing and timing the actions that are best poised for achieving the organization's goals," p. 2.

85 Porter and Kramer (2011), p. 66.

86 Simons (2013), pp. 31–32.

CHAPTER 7: The Valuation of Firms Should Be a Continual Learning Process

87 Barton (2011), p. 85. In addition, see fclt.org, which is the website for Focusing Capital on the Long Term—an initiative for advancing practical actions to focus business and investors on the long term.

88 Madden (1999), pp. 109–10 and 253–54.

89 Ibid., pp. 105–42, and Holland and Matthews, forthcoming.

90 See Chapter 4 and Appendix A of Madden (1999). Later academic work on an implied discount rate, e.g., Gebhardt, Lee, and Swaminathan (2001), did not benefit from using a large universe of firms with explicit fade forecasts based on past firm characteristics as employed by the Credit Suisse HOLT global database.

91 The empirical findings in Madden (1999), pp. 165–67, were later replicated by Credit Suisse HOLT using more refined econometric techniques for long-term time periods, including U.S. and non-U.S. firms. See also Fama and French (2000), Wiggins and Ruefli (2002), (2005), and Kengelbach, Grand, and Roos (2007). Fama and French (1999) estimated, for the period 1950-1996, that the real cost of capital was 5.95 percent and the real return on corporate assets was 7.38 percent.

92 Ng, Jhaveri, and Graziano (2006).

93 See Healy, Myers, and Howe (2002) for a simulation study that is in the spirit of the model corporation.

94 Figure 7.5 was developed by Rawley Thomas. See his 2013 book *Valu-Focus Investing: A Cash-Loving Contrarian Way to Invest in Stocks* for an application of the life-cycle framework to investing.

CHAPTER 8: The Quest for High Performance and Concluding Thoughts

95 Erhard and Jensen (2014). For an overview of their collaboration focused on leadership, see beingaleader.net.

96 Rosenzweig (2007), p. 120.

97 Ibid., p. 122.

98 Beasley (1948), p. 90.

99 Taylor and Schroeder (2003), pp. 73-74.

100 Smith (2016).

101 Bossidy and Charan (2002), pp. xxiii–xxxi, list seven essential behaviors in order to execute well: know your people and know your business, insist on realism, identify clear goals and priorities, follow through, reward the doers, expand people's capabilities, and know yourself.

REFERENCES

Adner, Ron. 2012. *The Wide Lens: What Successful Innovators See That Others Miss.* New York: Penguin Group.

Allison, John A. 2013. *The Financial Crisis and the Free Market Cure: Why Pure Capitalism Is the World Economy's Only Hope.* New York: McGraw Hill.

———. 2015. *The Leadership Crisis and the Free Market Cure: Why the Future of Business Depends on the Return to Life, Liberty, and the Pursuit of Happiness.* New York: McGraw Hill.

Amabile, Teresa, and Steven Kramer. 2011. *The Progress Principle: Using Small Wins to Ignite Joy, Engagement, and Creativity at Work.* Boston: Harvard Business Review Press.

Barrett, Louise. 2011. *Beyond the Brain: How Body and Environment Shape Animal and Human Minds.* Princeton: Princeton University Press.

Barton, Dominic. 2011. "Capitalism for the Long Term." *Harvard Business Review* March 2011: 85–91.

Baumol, William J. 2002. *The Free-Market Innovation Machine: analyzing the growth miracle of capitalism.* Princeton: Princeton University Press.

Bazin, Hervé. 2000. *The Eradication of Smallpox.* London: Academic Press.

Beasley, Norman. 1948. *Main Street Merchant: The Story of J. C. Penney*

Company. New York: McGraw Hill.

Bessen, James. 2015. *Learning by Doing: The Real Connection between Innovation, Wages, and Wealth*. New Haven: Yale University Press.

Bezos, Jeff. 2008. "Bezos on Innovation." Interview. *Bloomberg Business* April 16, 2008.

Bezos, Jeffrey P. 1997. Shareholder letter for Amazon's 1997 annual report, available at Amazon.com.

———. 2011. Shareholder letter for Amazon's 2011 annual report, available at Amazon.com.

Bhidé, Amar. 2008. *The Venturesome Economy: How Innovation Sustains Prosperity in a More Connected World*. Princeton: Princeton University Press.

Bortoft, Henri. 2012. *Taking Appearance Seriously: The Dynamic Way of Seeing in Goethe and European Thought*. Edinburgh: Floris Books.

Bossidy, Larry, and Ram Charan. 2002. *Execution: The Discipline of Getting Things Done*. London: Random House.

Bower, Joseph L., Herman B. Leonard, and Lynn S. Paine. 2011. *Capitalism at Risk: Rethinking the Role of Business*. Boston: Harvard Business Review Press.

Brayer, Elizabeth. 2006. *George Eastman: A Biography*. Rochester, NY: University of Rochester Press.

Brothers, Chalmers. 2005. *Language and the Pursuit of Happiness*. Naples, FL: New Possibilities Press.

Carey, Timothy A. 2006. *The Method of Levels*. Hayward, CA: Living Control Systems Publishing.

Christensen, Clayton M., and Stephen P. Kaufman. 2008. "Assessing Your Organization's Capabilities: Resources, Processes, and Priorities." *Harvard Business School Module Note.* August 21, 2008.

Christensen, Clayton M., and Derek van Bever. 2014. "The Capitalist's Dilemma." *Harvard Business Review.* June: 60–68.

Colander, David, and Roland Kupers. 2014. *Complexity and the Art of Public Policy: Solving Society's Problems from, the Bottom Up.* Princeton: Princeton University Press.

Collins, Jim. 2001. *Good to Great: Why Some Companies Make the Leap ... And Others Don't.* New York: HarperBusiness.

Comfort, Mildred Houghton. 1962. *William L. McKnight, Industrialist.* Minneapolis: T. S. Denison & Company.

Corrado, Carol, John Haltiwanger, and Daniel Sichel. 2005. *Measuring Capital in the New Economy.* Chicago: University of Chicago Press.

Cosgrove, Toby. 2014. *The Cleveland Clinic Way: Lessons in Excellence from One of the World's Leading Healthcare Organizations.* New York: McGraw Hill.

Cox, James F., and John G. Schleier, Jr., eds. 2010. *Theory of Constraints Handbook.* New York: McGraw-Hill.

Cziko, Gary. 2000. *The Things We Do: Using the Lessons of Bernard and Darwin to Understand the What, How, and Why of Our Behavior.* Cambridge, MA: MIT Press.

DeLuzio, Mark. 2001. "Danaher Is a Paragon of Lean Success." Interview. *Manufacturing News* June 29, 2001.

Donaldson, Gordon. 1995. "A New Tool for Boards: The Strategic Audit." *Harvard Business Review* (July/August): 990–1007.

Eccles, Robert G., and Michael P. Krzus. 2015. *The Integrated Reporting Movement: Meaning, Momentum, Motives, and Materiality.* Hoboken, NJ: John Wiley & Sons.

Eccles, Robert G., and Nitn Nohria. 1992. *Beyond the Hype: Rediscovering the Essence of Management.* Cambridge, MA: Harvard Business School Press.

Erhard, Werner, and Michael Jensen. 2014. "Putting Integrity into Finance." *Rotman Management* Spring 2014: 19–23.

Fama, Eugene F., and Kenneth R. French. 1999. "The Corporate Cost of Capital and the Return on Corporate Investment." *Journal of Finance* 54(6): 1939-67.

Fama, E. F., and K. R. French. 2000. "Forecasting Profitability and Earnings." *Journal of Business* 73(2): 161–75.

Fernandez, Pablo. 2015. *Valuation and Common Sense.* 5th edition. Available at ssrn.com/abstract=2209089.

Forssell, Dag, ed. 2009. *Perceptual Control Theory: Science & Applications, A Book of Readings.* Hayward, CA: Living Control Systems Publishing.

Friedman, Milton. 1970. "The Social Responsibility of Business Is to Increase its Profits." *New York Times Magazine* September 13, 1970.

Frigo, Mark L., and Joel Litman. 2007. *Driven: Business Strategy, Human Actions, and the Creation of Wealth.* Chicago: Strategy & Execution, LLC.

Frigo, Mark L., and Mark C. Ubelhart. 2015. "CFO+CHRO=POWER PAIR." *Strategic Finance* November 2015.

———. 2016. "Human Capital Management: The Central Element of All Risk." *People + Strategy* Winter 2016.

Frith, Chris. 2007. *Making Up the Mind: How the Brain Creates Our Mental World*. Hoboken, NJ: John Wiley & Sons.

Fuller, Joseph, and Michael C. Jensen. 2002. "Just Say No to Wall Street: Putting a stop to the Earnings Game." *Journal of Applied Corporate Finance* 14(4): 41–46.

Gebhardt, William R., Charles M. C. Lee, and Bhaskaran Swaminathan. 2001. "Toward an Implied Cost of Capital." *Journal of Accounting Research* 39(1): 135–76.

George, Bill. 2003. *Authentic Leadership: Rediscovering the Secrets to Creating Lasting Value*. San Francisco: Jossey-Bass.

Gerstner, Louis V. 2002. *Who Says Elephants Can't Dance?: Inside IBM's Historic Turnaround*. New York: HarperBusiness.

Glass, Ira. 2010. Radio interview 403: NUMMI transcript. *This American Life* from WBEZ, March 26, 2010.

Goldratt, Eliyahu M., and Jeff Cox. 1984. *The Goal: A Process of Ongoing Improvement*. Great Barrington, MA: North River Press.

Goldratt, Eliyahu M., and Efrat Goldratt-Ashlag. 2008. *The Choice*. Great Barrington, MA: North River Press.

Graham, John R., Campbell R. Harvey, and Shivaram Rajgopal. 2006. "Value Destruction and Financial Reporting Decisions." *Financial Analysts Journal* 62, 6 (November/December): 27–39.

Gregory, Richard L. 2009. *Seeing Through Illusions*. Oxford: Oxford University Press.

Guiso, Luigi, Paola Sapienza, and Luigi Zingales. 2013. "The Value of Corporate Culture." Booth Working Paper No. 13-80, September 2013.

Gundling, Ernest. 2000. *The 3M Way to Innovation: Balancing People and Profit*. Toyko: Kodanska International.

Hand, John, and Baruch Lev. 2003. *Intangible Assets: Values, Measures, and Risks*. Oxford: Oxford University Press.

Hanushek, Eric A., and Ludger Woessmann. 2015. *The Knowledge Capital of Nations*. Cambridge, MA: MIT Press.

Healy, Paul M., Stewart C. Myers, and Christopher D. Howe. 2002. "R&D Accounting and the Tradeoff Between Relevance and Objectivity." *Journal of Accounting Research* 40(3): 677–710.

Hess, Edward D. 2014. *Learn or Die: Using Science to Build a Leading-Edge Learning Organization*. New York: Columbia University Press.

Hindo, Brian. 2007. "At 3M, a Struggle between Efficiency and Creativity." *Bloomberg BusinessWeek*. June 10, 2007.

Holland, David, and Bryant Matthews. forthcoming. *Beyond Earnings*. Hoboken, NJ: John Wiley & Sons.

Israel, Paul. 1998. *Edison: A Life of Invention*. New York: John Wiley & Sons, Inc.

Jensen, Michael C. 2001. "Value Maximization, Stakeholder Theory, and the Corporate Objective Function." *Journal of Applied Corporate Finance* 14(3): 8–21.

———. 2009. "Integrity: Without It Nothing Works." *Rotman Magazine* Fall 2009: 16–20.

Jensen, Michael C., and Joe Fuller. 2003. "What's a Director to Do?" In *Best Practices: Ideas and Insights from the World's Foremost Business Thinkers*. Cambridge, MA: Perseus Publishing.

Johnson, H. Thomas. 2007. "Lean Dilemma: Choose System Principles or Management Accounting Controls—Not Both." In Joe Stenzel, ed., *Lean Accounting: Best Practices for Sustainable Integration.* Hoboken, NJ: John Wiley & Sons.

Kahneman, Daniel. 2011. *Thinking Fast and Slow.* New York: Farrar, Straus and Giroux.

Kahneman, Daniel, and Gary Klein. 2009. "Conditions for Intuitive Expertise." *American Psychologist* 64(6): 515–26.

Kengelbach, Jens, Hans le Grand, and Alexander Roos. 2007. "Performance of abnormal returns and possible applications for company valuation." SSRN working paper ssrn.com/abstract=1002041.

Klein, Gary. 2013. *Seeing What Others Don't: The Remarkable Ways We Gain Insights.* New York: Public Affairs.

Koch, Charles G. 2015. *Good Profit: How Creating Value for Others Built One of the World's Most Successful Companies.* New York: Crown Business.

Larish, John J. 2012. *Out of Focus: The story of how Kodak lost its direction.* Published by the author.

Lev, Baruch. 2012. *Winning Investors Over: Surprising Truths About Honesty, Earnings Guidance, and Other Ways to Boost Your Stock Price.* Boston: Harvard Business Review Press.

Lev, Baruch, Suresh Radhakrishnan, and Peter C. Evans. 2016. "Organizational Capital: A CEO's Guide to Measuring and Managing Enterprise Intangibles." Center for Global Enterprise, January 2015.

Mackey, John. 2005. Comments made as part of a debate, "Rethinking the Social Responsibility of Business." October 1, 20005. available at reason.com/archives.

Mackey, John, and Raj Sisodia. 2013. *Conscious Capitalism*. Boston: Harvard Business Review Press.

Madden, Bartley J. 1991. "A Transactional Approach to Economic Research." *Journal of Socio-Economics* 20(1): 57–71. Available at learningwhatworks.com/papers/transactional%20approach.pdf.

———. 1999. *CFROI Valuation: A Total System Approach to Valuing the Firm*. Oxford: Butterworth-Heinemann.

———. 2007a. "For Better Corporate Governance, the Shareholder Value Review." *Journal of Applied Corporate Finance* 19(1): 102—14

———. 2007b. "Guidepost to Wealth Creation: Value-Relevant Track Records." *Journal of Applied Finance* 17(2): 119–30.

———. 2008. "Shareholder Value Reviews." *Strategic Finance* (September): 16–20.

———. 2011. "Management's Knowing Process and the Theory of Constraints." Working paper available at ssrn.com/abstract=1806500.

———. 2012a. "Management's Worldview: Four Critical Points about Reality, Language, and Knowledge Building." *Journal of Organizational Computing and Electronic Commerce*. 22(4): 334–46.

———. 2012b. *Free to Choose Medicine: Better Drugs Sooner at Lower Cost*, 2nd ed. Naperville, IL: LearningWhatWorks.

———. 2014. *Reconstructing Your Worldview: The Four Core Beliefs You Need to Solve Complex Business Problems*. Naperville, IL: LearningWhatWorks.

Mansell, Warren, and Timothy A. Carey. 2009. "A century of psychology and psychotherapy: Is an understanding of 'control' the missing link between theory, research, and practice?" *Psychology and Psychotherapy: Theory, Research, and Practice* 82: 337–53.

Marken, Richard S. 1992. *Mind Readings: Experimental Studies of Purpose.* Durango, CO: Control Systems Group.

———. 2002. *More Mind Readings: Methods and Models in the Study of Purpose.* St. Louis, MO: newview.

McClelland, Kent A., and Thomas J. Fararo, eds. 2006. *Purpose, Meaning, and Action.* New York: Palgrave Macmillan.

McCloskey, Dierdre N. 2010. *Bourgeois Dignity: Why Economics Can't Explain The Modern World.* Chicago: University of Chicago Press.

Merlino, James. 2015. *Service Fanatics: How to Build Superior Patient Experience the Cleveland Clinic Way.* New York: McGraw Hill.

Neffinger, John, and Matthew Kohut. 2013. *Compelling People: The Hidden Qualities That Make Us Influential.* New York: Penguin Group.

Ng, Chiew Leng, Viral Jhaveri, and Ron Graziano. 2006. "HOLT Taiwan: Accounting for Employee Stock Bonus." Credit Suisse HOLT research report, December 5, 2006.

Nordhaus, William D. 2004. "Schumpeterian Profits in the American Economy: Theory and Measurement." NBER Working Paper 10433, April 2004.

Phelps, Edmund. 2013. *Mass Flourishing: How Grassroots Innovation Created Jobs, Challenge, and Change.* Princeton, NJ: Princeton University Press.

Philipson, Tomas J., and Anupam B. Jena. 2006. "Surplus Appropriation from R&D and Health Care Technology Asesment Procedures." NBER Working Paper 12016, January 2006.

Porter, Michael E., and Mark R. Kramer. 2011. "Creating Shared Value." *Harvard Business Review* January-February 2011: 62–77.

Powers, William T. 1989. *Living Control Systems*. Gravel Switch, KY: Control Systems Group.

———. 1992. *Living Control Systems II*. Gravel Switch, KY: Control Systems Group.

———. 1998. *Making Sense of Behavior*. New Canaan, CT: Benchmark Publications.

———. 2001. "The Neglected Phenomenon of Negative Feedback Control." LivingControlSystems.com/intro_papers/neglected_phenomenon.pdf.

———. 2005. *Behavior: The Control of Perception*. New Canaan, CT: Benchmark Publications.

———. 2008. *Living Control Systems III: The Fact of Control*. Bloomfield, NJ: Benchmark Publications.

Rajan, Raghuram G., and Luigi Zingales. 2003. *Saving Capitalism from the Capitalists: Unleashing the Power of Financial Markets to Create Wealth and Spread Opportunity*. New York: Crown Business.

Ridley, Matt. 2010. *The Rational Optimist: How Prosperity Evolves*. New York: Harper Collins.

Robinson, Simon, and Maria Moraes Robinson. 2014. *Holonomics: Business Where People and Planet Matter*. Glasgow: Floris Books.

Rodriguez, Ana Maria. 2006. *Edward Jenner: Conqueror of Smallpox*. Berkeley Heights, NJ: Enslow Publishers.

Rose, Dwight C. 1928a. "Common Stocks at the Current Price Level." Joint annual meeting of the American Statistical Association and the American Economic Association. December 27, 1928.

————. 1928b. *A Scientific Approach to Investment Management.* New York: Harper & Brothers Publishers.

Rosenzweig, Phil. 2007. *The Halo Effect ... and the Eight Other Business Delusions that Deceive Managers.* New York: Free Press.

Rother, Mike. 2010. *Toyota Kata: Managing People for Improvement, Adaptiveness, and Superior Results.* New York: McGraw Hill.

Rumelt, Richard P. 2011. *Good Strategy Bad Strategy: The Difference and Why It Matters.* New York: Crown Business.

Runkel, Philip J. 2003. *People as Living Things: The Psychology of Perceptual Control.* Hayward, CA: Living Control Systems Publishing.

Schein, Edgar H. 2010. *Organizational Culture and Leadership.* 4th ed. Hoboken, NJ: Jossey-Bass.

Senge, Peter M. 2006. *The Fifth Discipline: The Art & Practice of the Learning Organization.* New York: Doubleday.

Shook, John. 2010. "How to Change a Culture: Lessons from NUMMI." *MIT Sloan Management Review* Winter 2010: 63–68.

Simons, Robert. 2013. "The Business of Business Schools: Restoring a Focus on Competing to Win." *Capitalism and Society* 8(1), Article 2.

Smith, Brad. 2016. "The Most Important Job of a CEO." investors.intuit.com, accessed March 13, 2016.

Soto, Hernando de. 1989. *The Other Path: The Invisible Revolution in the Third World.* New York: Harper & Row.

————. 2003. *The Mystery of Capitalism: Why Capitalism Triumphs in the West and Fails Everywhere Else.* New York: Basic Books.

Stewart, Bennet G. 2013. *Best-Practice EVA: The Definitive Guide to Measuring and Maximizing Shareholder Value.* Hoboken, NJ: John Wiley & Sons.

Stigler, George. 1963. *Capital and Rates of Return in Manufacturing Industries.* Princeton, NJ: Princeton University Press.

Stone, Brad. 2013. *The Everything Store: Jeff Bezos and the Age of Amazon.* New York: Back Bay Books.

Taylor, Suzanne, and Kathy Schroeder. 2003. *Inside Intuit: How the Makers of Quicken Beat Microsoft and Revolutionized an Entire Industry.* Boston: Harvard Business School Press.

Tett, Gillian. 2015. *The Silo Effect: The Peril of Expertise and the Promise of Breaking Down Barriers.* New York: Simon & Schuster.

Thomas, Rawley, and William Mahoney. 2013. *ValuFocus Investing: A Cash-Loving Contrarian Way to Invest in Stocks.* Hoboken, NJ: John Wiley & Sons.

Timmerman, Luke. 2015. "DNA Sequencing Market Will Exceed $20 Billion, Says Illumina CEO Jay Flatley." *Forbes* interview. April 29, 2015.

Tong, Jamie Y., and Feida (Frank) Zhang. 2014. "More Evidence that Corporate R&D Investment (and Effective Boards) Can Increase Firm Value." *Journal of Applied Corporate Finance* 26(2): 94–100.

Ubelhart, Mark C. 2009. "An Economic View of the Impact of Human Capital on Firm Performance and Valuation." In Thomas, Rawley, and Benton Gup. Eds. 2009. *The Valuation Handbook: Valuation Techniques from Today's Top Practitioners.* Hoboken, NJ: John Wiley & Sons.

Walton, Sam. 1992. *Sam Walton: Made in America: My Story.* New York: Doubleday.

Wiggins, Robert R., and Timothy W. Ruefli. 2002. "Sustained Competitive Advantage: Temporal Dynamics and the Incidence and Persistence of

Superior Economic Performance." *Organization Science* 13(1): 82–105.

———. 2005. "Schumpeter's Ghost: Is Hyper-competition Making the Best of Times Shorter?" *Strategic Management Journal* 26(10): 887–911.

Womack, James P., and Daniel T. Jones. 2003. *Lean Thinking: Banish Waste and Create Wealth in Your Corporation*, 2nd ed. New York: Free Press.

Womack, Jim. 2011. *Gemba Walks*. Cambridge, MA: Lean Enterprise Institute.

Yin, Henry H. "Restoring Purpose in Behavior." In Baldassarre, Gianluca, and Marco Mirolli, eds. 2013. *Computational and Robotic Models of the Hierarchical Organization of Behavior*. New York: Springer.

Zaffron, Steve, and Dave Logan. 2009. *The Three Laws of Performance: Rewriting the Future of Your Organization and Your Life*. San Francisco: Jossey-Bass.

Zapolski, Nancy, and Joe DiMaggio. 2011. *Insights and Distinctions*. San Francisco: Landmark Worldwide.

54941919R00134

Made in the USA
Lexington, KY
03 September 2016